Mid-Life Career Rescue

The Call for Change

How to Confidently Leave a Job You Hate and
Start Living a Life You Love, Before It's Too Late

Cassandra Gaisford, BCA, Dip Psych

Cover by Ida Fia Sveningsson

Published by Blue Giraffe Publishing 2015
Revised and updated 2017

Blue Giraffe Publishing is a division of Worklife Solutions Ltd.
www.worklifesolutions.nz

See our complete catalogue at www.worklifesolutions.nz

ISBN 978-0-9941314-0-9
First Edition

The tiny, brilliantly colored hummingbird
symbolizes the messages in this book.

This versatile soul, despite its size,
is capable of unbelievable feats.
It can hover in mid-air, fly forwards, backwards,
side-ways, and even upside down.
Its rapidly beating wings can flap as high as 200 times per
second,
enabling it to travel faster than a car.

The laws of physics say it should be impossible.
But the hummingbird does it anyway.

I dedicate this book to those of you
who are ready to live a life more colorful,
and to do what others may say cannot be done.

This book is also for Lorenzo, my Templar Knight,
who encourages and supports me
to make my dreams possible...

And for all my clients
who've shared their dreams with me,
and allowed me to help them achieve incredible feats.

Thank you
for inspiring me.

FREE WORKBOOK!

Thank you for your interest in my new book *Mid-Life Career Rescue*.

To show my appreciation, I'm excited to be giving you another book for FREE!

Download the free *Find Your Passion Workbook* here: http://worklifesolutions.leadpages.co/free-find-your-passion-workbook

I hope you enjoy it—it's dedicated to helping you live and work with passion.

CONTENTS

FOREWORD

In June 2009, I was listening to Paul Potts, winner of the 2007 Britain's Got Talent show, being interviewed by Steve Wright on BBC Radio 2 on his Big Show. When Paul appeared on Britain's Got Talent, he was working selling mobile phones, but astonished the judges and the audience with his incredible voice. He now tours the world wowing audiences with his voice.

Steve Wright asked Paul whether he loved singing as a child, or whether he came to singing in later life. Paul responded, "Yes, I'd always loved singing when I was young." So Steve then asked him why he ended up selling mobile phones rather than singing professionally, Paul answered by saying, "No-one ever told me when I was growing up that something I loved could be a career."

Most of us can relate to that: doing something you loved and then getting paid for it simply wasn't a career option that we were aware of or encouraged into. Too many of us believe that work needs to be a relentless and life long activity doing something we'd rather not be doing, but that we have little choice over. We just have to do it to survive. And as long we are not enjoying it, are suffering, bored, stressed or are sacrificing ourselves, then that is real work, and we deserve to be paid for it.

Too few of us have been bought up to believe that it is possible to make our living doing something we love, that lights our hearts up and stirs our passions. This I call the work we were born to do and is our true work. To find your true work is a great blessing, one of life's greatest blessings I believe. And to be paid for your work rather than work for pay is one of life's great joys.

More and more people today, either through choice or necessity, are looking for new and more fulfilling ways of working and earning their livings. Old ways are breaking down. Today, sacrificing your deeper passions for the security of a pay-check is no guarantee of security. Following your heart and deeper self is the new security. Your heart is the well-spring of possibility and opportunity that will never run dry.

In this book, Cassandra helps you find your work, inspiring you to consider new possibilities, gently guiding you beyond limiting thinking, and helping you find your own true self and authentic work.

Those who have found what they were born to do have usually developed a generosity of spirit and want to hold a hand out to others who are still searching. In this book, Cassandra has done just that.

Out of the blessings she has won for herself, she shares generously with you where to look, and what signposts to follow. She guides you to trust yourself to be able to bring your inner and outer worlds together, so that now you can make your living in a way that reflects who you are and what is precious to you.

Enjoy this book and let it guide you to the work that is in your heart to do.

—Nick Williams, Author of *The Work We Were Born to Do: Find the Work You Love, Love the Work You Do*

INTRODUCTION

All we need to make us really happy is something to be passionate about.

Do you feel trapped in a job that pays the bills but fails to give you a buzz?

Do you yearn for something more from your work and your life but can't see any alternatives?

Have you ever been told it is unrealistic to expect job satisfaction?

Are you feeling uninspired, lost and uncertain about what you can offer and how you might move forward?

Deep down do you feel you're too old to change, or trapped by your current circumstances?

Perhaps you're a mum returning to work, or you've been made redundant and looking for a new job.

Maybe you're still trying to figure out what you want to be 'when you grow up.' Or how to make a meaningful contribution as you contemplate retirement.

Whatever your reasons for needing a rescue, you're not alone.

Statistical research repeatedly confirms that well over half the workforce is unhappy, with Gallup's 2015 poll revealing only 13 percent of employees worldwide are happily engaged at work.

Many people feel stuck because they can't see any better options or don't know how to deal with obstacles preventing them from finding their best-fit career. Others lack the confidence and energy to make a positive change. Many stay stuck in jobs that don't fulfil them.

Perhaps you haven't had the time to sit down and think consciously about your career choices. Maybe like many mid-lifers you 'just fell into' your work. Or perhaps, you've made your choices based on other people's expectations.

I felt so unhappy at work once it made me sick, but I felt I had to make that job work or I'd be fired. I was a single mum, the only one able to support my young daughter and myself. I used to go home with a brave face, but inside I was tired and depressed. My self-esteem was so low I thought no one would hire me. I tried to go to work, grit my teeth and bare it.

I wanted to make a difference in people's lives. But that wasn't what my boss wanted from me. "You could make a lot of money here," he said. "You just need to be more selfish." For a while I tried to be someone else—motivated only by money, but everyday my values were compromised, and the skills I loved weren't used.

My job started making me ill. It got so bad I got shingles—a painful virus affecting the central nervous system. I felt trapped and unable to leave. My colleagues at work had similar experiences. It really was such a toxic workplace. Several people had heart attacks, and the amount of alcohol people consumed after work to numb the pain was staggering. I needed a career rescue. In desperation, I agreed to see a career counsellor. During my first session I was asked to draw a picture. I drew a grey bird in a black cage. "The door is open, but she's forgotten how to fly," I told her. This drawing brought tears to her eyes. Although I didn't understand why at the time, I can see now that she felt my pain at feeling so caught and trapped by my situation.

Through our sessions and the structured exercises we completed together I rebuilt my confidence and strengthened my awareness of my skills, and most importantly, I learned how to dream.

The work the career counsellor did with me was so important, so vital—saving me from despair. It led me to not just finding a job I loved, but later creating one that gave me a sense of purpose.

What she taught me literally gave me my life back. Happily, I can now serve others in this way too—as an author, qualified holistic energy psychologist, career counsellor, life and career coach, and a trainer of other coaches who also aspire to make a difference in other people's lives.

You and I are probably alike. I'm a mid-lifer who wants more from my life than to go work, grit my teeth and bare it. I want to work with joy, passion, purpose and fulfilment—and I still want to pay the bills!

I'm grateful to say that I've achieved all of those desires, and more. I've reinvented my working life multiple times in the search for career nirvana and I'm happy to say I've found it.

Equally as satisfying is the fact I've been able to share what I've learned and have helped thousands of people from a myriad of diverse backgrounds and circumstances find or create work they love and enjoy their lives.

I'm the founder of an internationally successful career and life coaching business and the author of a vast library of personal empowerment programs. I enjoy what I call a career combo—coaching, counselling, training, writing, public speaking...and a few other creative things I do on the side. Like writing historical art-related novels, painting and photography. And I've had the joy and privilege of helping thousands of people successfully reinvent their careers and lives.

I know what it's like to feel trapped. I know what it's like to doubt you'll ever be able to make a change for the better. I know what it's like to feel down, stressed and anxious. I know that in today's world when finding work is harder than ever, finding a job you love can feel like an impossible dream. I know it's possible!

Perhaps you're like Mandy who felt stuck in a job that paid the bills but was low on fun, joy, challenge and fulfilment. Or is your job, like Keith's—so insecure you don't think it will last? Do you yearn, like Matt, for something more from your work and your life but can't see any alternative options?

Deep down do you feel trapped, hopeless, sick? That was me. And it has been many of my clients. Once. But not anymore. And this book is designed to rescue you from unfulfilling work and show you how to break free of a job you hate and confidently find one you love.

Like Matt, then aged 58, who after reading this book left his job as a fed-up account director and started his own business. "*Mid-Life Career Rescue* has you thinking about what drives you, why you are doing what you are doing, is it making me happy, am I using my full set of skills, what can I do differently and how can I change?"

Thousands of people, many of them mid-lifers, like you, have been rescued from unfulfilling work, changed careers and found their dream jobs by implementing the tips and strategies found in this book.

What you're about to read isn't another self-help book; it's a self-empowerment book. If you're like many mid-lifers and still operating from antiquated and disempowering beliefs, the information in this book will help change your mindset. It offers ways to increase your self-knowledge. From that knowledge comes the power to take control of your life.

It is my sincerest hope that you will come to discover that many of the beliefs impacting your life are false and self-limiting and you'll be inspired and feel empowered to change these beliefs.

This Book Is Powerful

This book is powerful. I know it is. The life I have created using this awareness is amazing. The strategies are ones I have successfully used—professionally with clients and personally during numerous self-determined or sometimes forced reinventions.

I stand by every one of the strategies you will learn here, not just because they are grounded in strong theoretical principles, but also because I have used them to create successful turnaround, after successful turnaround in nearly every area of my life.

Mid-Life Career Rescue is the culmination of all that I have experienced and all that I have learned, applied and successfully taught others for over two decades. I don't practice what I preach; I preach what I have practiced—because it gets results.

One thing I know for certain is that your life is too important to stay in a job you hate. You have treasures buried within you—extraordinary treasures—and so do I, and so do others. And bringing those treasures to light takes faith and focus and courage and effort. It takes a willingness to answer the call for change, and people to help and support you along the way. People like me.

Why I Wrote This Book

Someone once asked me, "What was the catalyst for writing this particular book?" In part, it was my experience with clients, but also the emails I received from people who I knew would never be able to see me professionally, and their depth of hopelessness and despair—despair that reached beyond the individual, but affected those who loved them.

Like the lady who emailed me, "No one will employ my husband because he was 55 and had been in the same job for 25 years until he was made redundant. He keeps being told that he has no skills employers would want."

It broke my heart every time I had to reply to emails like this with, "I'm sorry we are not taking new clients at this time." Because I knew from experience it didn't have to be that way. I knew what he needed to learn was how to find his passion and clarify what gave him a sense of meaning and purpose, and how to sell his age and experience as an asset.

It was the experience of this man and many others like him that resulted in my decision to write my first book *Happy at Work for Mid-Lifers*. And it was the success and the feedback from those that read it that that led me to release a revised and updated version as *Mid-Life Career Rescue.*

As a recruitment consultant, I've seen first-hand how employers and recruiters can be ageist when it comes to hiring decisions. As a coach, I've helped people overcome this and get hired.

I've also seen people put self-imposed limits on what they believe is possible at their age. Even non-mid-lifers do that! "Don't you do what you love when you retire," one 28-year-old once said to me! "I'm too old to change, "said another man in his early thirties. I've helped people successfully challenge those limits.

As a career coach and counsellor helping mid-lifers reclaim their lives after redundancy, rebuild self-esteem after workplace bullying, and bounce back from the depression that staying in the wrong job can create, I felt strongly that people needed both practical and inspirational ways to reclaim their lives.

I also believe that people need fewer check boxes and career assessment inventories and more creative, out-of-the box thinking to help them succeed. My views resonated with many—and I was interviewed on television and on the radio about this very thing. You can check these out on my media page here: http://www.worklifesolutions.nz/media

I have also presented my unique Passion Driven Model of career design at conferences around the world. I'm not saying these things to boast—but to reassure you that you're in safe hands.

When I attended an international symposium of career practitioners in Venice, Italy, we were warned of the crisis an ageing workforce presented and were told that the greatest skill career coaches needed was—wait for it...

to help people have an imagination!

As an artist and creative soul, that was like candy to a child. And since then, I've proven over and over again, with the successes I've gained for clients that thinking differently and creatively, as well as rationally, while also harnessing the power of intuition, and applying the principles of manifestation, really works. In this book I'll show you why and how.

A large part of my philosophy, and the reason behind my success with clients, is my fervent belief that to achieve anything worthy in life you need to follow your passion. And I'm in good company.

As Oprah Winfrey said, "Passion is energy. Feel the power that comes from focusing on what excites you." Without passion, you don't have energy, and without energy you have nothing. You have to let desire, not fear, propel you forward. Yet worryingly, research suggests that less than 10% of people are following their passion. Perhaps that is why there is so much unhappiness at work.

Setting You Up For Success

"Aren't you setting people up for failure?" a disillusioned career coach once challenged me when I told her my focus was not on helping people find any job, but finding one that gave them joy. I couldn't help but wonder if she needed a career change.

Twenty-five years' cumulative professional experience as a career coach and counsellor, helping people work with passion and still pay the bills, answers that question. I'm setting people up for success. I'm not saying it will happen instantly, but if you follow the advice in this book, it will happen. I promise.

Your Life Is Waiting

"I've spent 40 years looking out of the window wishing I was somewhere else," one of my clients told me. That's not only depressing but also such a huge waste of talent and precious time. Life's too short to spend days, weeks and years in a job that robs you of energy, zest and enthusiasm.

We spend over 3,000 hours a year at work, and when we're not at work we're thinking about it. Work-related issues are major sources of stress and career unhappiness. Left unresolved they can spill over into other areas of your life, infecting your relationships with colleagues, family and loved ones.

Don't waste another day feeling trapped. Don't be the person who spends a life of regret, or waits until they retire before they follow their passions. Don't be the person too afraid to make a change for the better, or who wishes they could lead a significant life. Make the change now. Before it's too late.

Your story can be like Mandy's, who in her 50's, after reading the predecessor to *Mid-Life Career Rescue* wrote to me and told me how the book had changed her life:

"To be honest, I couldn't put the book down—it was as though Cassandra had got inside my head and written it specifically for me! It helped me process the what/where questions I was asking myself and discussed all the aspects that had been tumbling around in my head like a washing machine for many months. It helped me process my thoughts, clarify my thinking, formulate a real plan and prepare myself for my new life."

And what a new life it was. Mandy packed up her old life as a disillusioned consultant and unhappy wife in New Zealand and moved to outback Australia after successfully applying for a new role. She landed a three-year contract as an Infrastructure and Assets Manager, overseeing the construction of the Art Centre and new houses, as well as the commercialization of the airport and the development of major roads.

"I wanted a new adventure and I've found one!" she wrote to me. "I'm excited and terrified." Others saw Mandy as an inspiration, paving the way for other mid-lifers to make courageous life and career changes.

My clients, and readers like Mandy, tell me they value the fact that my advice is gained from both my personal and professional experiences and is both practical and inspirational.

Keith was 55 when his position was made redundant after 38 years of loyal service. "The biggest thing I am dealing with is a hit to my self-worth," he wrote to me.

"I am a proponent of the law of attraction and have proved this law many times but that does not stop me having serious doubts about my ability to pull above the 'mind chatter'. Your book is a great resource for boosting my energy and confidence.

"Honestly, your book is a treasure. I have found it very useful in terms of the information provided and tools available for self awareness and future planning. This is an awesome book and one I would recommend to anyone looking to change their career, not just mid-lifers.

"I feel energized every time I pick it up and I go back and re-read sections I have already read. I thank you for your foresight in writing this book and the energy and enthusiasm you pass on through the book."

Reach For Your Dreams

Passion, happiness, joy, fulfilment, love—call it what you will but my deepest desire is that this book encourages you to reach for your dreams, to never settle, to believe in the highest aspirations you have for yourself. You have so many gifts, so many talents that the world so desperately needs. We need people like you who care about what they do, who want to live and work with passion and purpose.

My Promise

I promise that if you follow the steps in this book you'll discover what you really want to do, clarify what you can do, and create powerful but simple strategies to make your dream a reality.

And I promise you'll find a job that you love, one that adds more joy to your life and gives you a sense of meaning, purpose and fulfilment.

And what I can promise you is this—whatever your circumstances, it's never too late to re-create yourself and your life. So, what are you waiting for? The clock is ticking, and the world is spinning, and you simply do not have time anymore to waste. It's time to start living a life you love, before it's too late.

The practical and inspirational tips and strategies you're about to read have been proven to create positive results, and provide knowledge that you can use again and again.

Be empowered. Answer the call for change, take control of your career and your life right now. As Steve Jobs once said, "Your time is limited." Make your life count, and enjoy the new future you're creating.

Let's get started.

THE CALL FOR CHANGE

"A human being is not one in pursuit of happiness but rather in search of a reason to be happy" ~ *Viktor Frankl, Psychiatrist and Author*

Irritability, boredom, fatigue, feelings of depression and other joyless experiences are classic signs that it's time to make a change. But many mid-lifers soldier on, ignoring the signs, or staying stuck in a role they have outgrown. They feel trapped in a rut because they don't know how to make a move.

It takes energy and effort, optimism and feelings of hope and excitement to summon the personal power to make a change for the better. It also takes a large dose of self-awareness and an ability to think laterally.

These things can feel in short supply when you're feeling discouraged, stuck in the comfort rut or so stressed out you can't see the wood for the forest. The exercises in *The Call For Change* will begin the process of helping you:

- Tune into the signs and boost awareness that it's time to change

- Identify the key causes of job dissatisfaction and begin identifying a cure

- Build a strong foundation for change by identifying, and managing stress and building greater resilience

- Gain greater clarity about what you want to change and how to direct your energies positively toward your preferred future

- Strengthen your creative thinking skills, and ability to identify possible roles you would enjoy

- Build hope and confirm there is no better time for you to change career.

Let's look briefly at which each chapter in this book will cover.

Where there is a problem there is a cure. Chapter One, "Unhappiness at Work," will help you identify the key causes of your job dissatisfaction. We will turn negatives into positives by adopting a solutions-focused approach to resolving current concerns.

This chapter will help you gain greater clarity about what you want to change and how to direct your energies positively toward your preferred future.

You'll gain greater insight into your personal passions, and criteria for job satisfaction. Knowing these things will help you begin the process of creating and attracting your dream role.

Research suggests that many mid-lifers have a negative expectancy about their ability to find meaningful work. Chapter Two, "The Gift of Longevity," will highlight the opportunities that demographic and social shifts have created for mature employees.

Activities in this chapter, and emphasizing age as an asset, will help strengthen your self-belief and confidence, and overcome any lingering doubts about re-inventing your life at your age and life stage. This will enable you to target your job-hunting activities positively.

Preparing for change and building a good, stable foundation by boosting and fortifying your health—mentally, physically, emotionally and spiritually, is an essential, and often neglected, component of successful career transitions.

Chapter Three, "Stress Less," will help you develop effective strategies to manage any current stress. Very often getting rid of stressors, and restoring some balance, can led you to fall back in love with your job.

It will also provide you with some useful tools to help you build resilience throughout the change process should you decide to make a move.

Traditional career paths are fast disappearing and the jobs of the future have yet to be invented. Chapter Four, "It All Begins with an Idea," highlights the role of creativity in defining and finding the work you want to do.

This chapter will introduce you to some creative, yet practical, techniques that will help you gain greater clarity about what inspires and excites you and begin the process of finding your best-fit career.

How To Use This Book

Mid-Life Career Rescue takes the stress out of changing careers by tapping into the power of creativity and out of the box thinking. Right from the start it will stretch your awareness of what you think is possible.

This book will help you make informed career choices that allow you to be true to yourself and that stand the test of time.

It provides a systematic, structured and inspirational way to facilitate both self—and career-awareness, and to help you have faith in yourself and confidence in your decisions.

The key components of determining what you want to do and what others will pay you to do are presented in bite-sized portions that make it much easier to assimilate.

Journal exercises, inspiring quotations and many other simple but effective tools to feed your inspiration and boost your confidence will help feed your desire for a new, improved life.

Throughout this book you'll be encouraged to make positive changes in your life, step by step, by applying the strategies discussed. You may want to create a special journal, notebook or use a digital tool to make a few notes and apply the tools and techniques I've designed especially for you.

My aim is to make *Mid-Life Career Rescue* as interactive as possible by combining a minimum of theory with a maximum of practical tools and techniques that you can apply to your own situation.

Your Virtual Coach

To really benefit from this book think of it as your 'virtual' coach—try the action tasks, and additional exercises that you'll find in all the chapters.

These action tasks are designed to facilitate greater insight and to help you integrate new learnings. Resist the urge to just process them in your head. We learn best by doing. Research has proven time and time again that the act of writing deepens your knowledge and learning.

Writing down your insights is the area where people like motivational guru Tony Robbins say that the winners part from the losers, because the losers always find a reason not to write things down. Harsh but perhaps true!

You will also come across plenty of action questions. Open-ended questions are great thought provokers. Your answers to these questions will help you gently challenge current assumptions and gain greater clarity about your goals and desires.

If you are currently unemployed, or not in the paid workforce, you may find it helpful to think about your previous roles when completing the exercises.

Keeping A Passion Journal

A passion journal is also a great place to store sources of inspiration to support you through the career planning and change process. For some tips to help you create your own inspirational passion journal, go to the media page on my website and watch my television interview here:

http://worklifesolutions.nz/media/tv-radio-and-youtube/

Passion Journal Tip Sheet

Every year I create a passion journal to help clarify and manifest my intentions. It's a fun and incredibly powerful process. I've created my dream job, a soul mate, our wonderful life style property, a publishing contract and more. Try it for yourself! Download my free tip sheet to help you create your own passion journal here:

www.worklifesolutions.nz/books/career-rescue

Inspirational Quotes

Sometimes all it takes is the slightest encouragement—one simple inspirational sentence—to launch oneself into a new and more satisfying orbit. I have included plenty of inspiration throughout the book and in the Career Rescue Community detailed below to help you do just that!

Surf The Net

Throughout the book I have included a selection of my e-Resources. These have been carefully selected to encourage further insight and to enable you to tap into regularly updated resources, including those created by me just for you.

There is no 'right' or 'wrong' way to work with *Mid-Life Career Rescue*. It's a very flexible tool—the only requirement is that you use it in a way that meets your needs. For example, you may wish to work through the book and exercises sequentially. Alternatively, you may wish to work intuitively and complete the exercises in an ad hoc fashion. Or just start where you need to start.

Whilst it is recommended that the chapters and the exercises are worked through in the order they appear, each chapter can be read independently. You may wish to read a chapter each week, fortnight or month. Or you may wish to use your intuition and select a page at random.

Web links throughout the book and the supplementary resources will help encourage further moments of insight, inspiration and clarity about the career path that's right for you.

Getting Started

Increasing your self-awareness is a crucial first step in moving toward the career of your dreams. Take the time to complete the following self-assessment quiz to evaluate where you are now.

Self-Assessment Quiz

1. You know where you want to be in 5-10 years' time

2. You have a clear idea of what gives your life meaning and purpose

3. You know what you are personally passionate about

4. You can quickly identify the three things which you spend the most time on in a week—work, kids, love, spirituality, health, relaxation, money, altruism, friendships

5. You can clearly identify your deepest, driving interests

6. You can clearly define your personal values

7. You know how your values apply to a variety of jobs and organizations

8. You know what your skills and talents are

9. You know what skills you enjoy using and that give you a buzz

10. You know how your skills and passions can transfer into different careers

11. You know who you are and what makes you tick

12. You have a strong level of self-awareness

13. You are in tune with your body barometer and recognize the signs your body gives you in response to stressful or passionate events

14. You know how to use your strengths to minimize your weaknesses

15. You can quickly and easily name three of your weaknesses, bad habits or behaviors that get on other people's nerves

16. You are clear about the things that hold you back and have developed a strategy to minimize these weaknesses

17. You can quickly name three activities that always relax and refresh you

18. You are clear about your preferred way of making decisions

19. At any point in time you can readily name your emotions, and use these intelligently to guide your decisions

20. You are aware how you may be influenced by the opinions of other people and take care to surround yourself with positive influences

21. You listen to your inner voice and act on your intuition

Scoring:

If you answered "yes" to 14 or more of these statements you have a great level of self-awareness and are really clear about what drives your career decisions.

If you answered "yes" to more than six but less than 14 of these statements, you are less aware of what drives your career decisions and would benefit from gaining more self-awareness about your own strengths and motivating forces.

If you answered "yes" to five or less of these statements a more focused effort to build awareness in those areas you answered "no" to will really help you build confidence and identify career options that you will enjoy and be good at.

Once you are clear about the forces that drive your decisions, finding a job that you like is easy. It won't happen overnight but it will happen! The exercises in the book will show you how.

Coping With Change

Unless we try to stretch beyond what we have already mastered we cannot grow.

We tend to be creatures of habit—to want guarantees and certainty before stepping forth into the unknown. This can make embarking on change challenging. Resisting the status quo or breaking free of the comfort rut takes considerable energy, determination and constant focus on the reasons why you want to change in the first place.

Have faith in yourself and your capacity for reinvention and remember you're not starting at the beginning. You already have a wealth of skills and knowledge, and life experience to draw upon.

The possibilities are endless—now more than ever you can be, do and have nearly anything you desire.

The key is to stay flexible and have fun—then re-inventing your career and your life can be a truly enlightening experience. Enjoy the journey and allow your passion to guide, motivate and inspire you.

Are you ready to heed the call for change?

UNHAPPINESS AT WORK

Sometimes in life, as in photography, you need a negative to make a positive image of the life you want to capture.

Are you showing signs of job dissatisfaction? Did you wake up this morning excited to face the day ahead? Or did the thought of getting up and going to work make you wish you could stay in bed?

If Monday mornings are a low point in your week, it may be a sign that it's time for a new career.

Often you know what you want subconsciously before you know it consciously. While you may still be debating whether or not to stay in your job, your subconscious mind may have already decided it's time for you to move on.

You may be like so many of my clients who say, "I could do anything if only I knew what it was."

The exercises in this chapter and those following will help take the stress out of making a change, confirm your best-fit career and give you the confidence to move toward your preferred future.

A good place to start is to use current things getting you down as signposts to your preferred future. Sometimes in life, as in photography, you need a negative to make a positive.

Confirming what's causing your job blues will help you get clear about your intentions, options and possibilities.

Perhaps you're like many of my clients and wonder whether you, not your job, are the major cause of your unhappiness. Is it your attitude? Or is it your work that's making you feel trapped? Getting clear about who you are and what you need to feel happy and fulfilled is an important step in confirming exactly which one needs to change.

Carlos Castaneda, in his book *The Fire From Within*, teaches Don Juan about the need to take care before embarking on change, when he says, "To have a path of knowledge, a path with heart makes for a joyful journey and is the only conceivable way to live. We must then think carefully about our paths before we set out on them for by the time a person discovers that his path 'has no heart,' the path is ready to kill him. At that point few of us have the courage to abandon the path, lethal as it may be, because we have invested so much in it, and to choose a new path seems so dangerous, even irresponsible. And so we continue dutifully, if joylessly along."

Tune Into Your Body Barometer

Liking what you do is not only a vital ingredient of career success but also health and mental well-being. When you don't do the things you love your health can suffer.

Common signs of neglecting your happiness and feeling trapped in a job that you don't enjoy can include:

- Headaches

- Insomnia

- Tiredness

- Depression

- Low self-esteem

- Lack of confidence

- Irritability and other warning signs.

You'll be able to identify your own warning signs in Chapter Three: Stress Less, and identify some strategies to boost your resilience. The main thing I want to emphasize is that your body never lies; however, many people soldier on ignoring the obvious warning signs their body is giving them—until it's too late.

It's easy to rationalize these feelings away, but the reality is your body is screaming out for something different. Something way better! Having the courage to say "Enough" and to pursue a more satisfying alternative can seem daunting but the rewards and benefits that flow make the effort so worthwhile.

Part of being a winner is knowing when to quit.

Action Questions

Why do you need a job that makes you happy? What benefits will flow when you are living your passion? What happens when you ignore your passion?

Some Alarming Facts:

- Less than 10% of people are visibly living their passion. Lack of passion and career dissatisfaction are common causes of stress, low productivity, poor performance and plummeting levels of confidence and self-esteem.

- Lack of feedback, autocratic bosses, poor work-life balance, lack of control, values conflicts, low challenge, boredom, high workloads and interpersonal conflicts push happiness levels down on a daily basis for a large number of employees.

- We all know that smoking kills but few people know that job strain is as bad as smoking according to researchers from the Harvard School of Public Health in Boston. They concluded that too often people rely on medication to tackle the job blues but one of the most effective cures would be to tackle the job environment.

- Unhappiness at work is a major drain on individuals, organizations and the economy. One Canadian study argued that a 1% improvement through helping people become fully engaged in programs that lead them to find work they would love, would release an additional $600 million each year into the economy.

- Many people have been conditioned to expect less from the world of work, and may have narrow expectations about the wealth of opportunity that now exists.

- Unhappy people complain more, produce less, get sick more often, worry more, have fewer creative ideas, have lower energy levels, are more pessimistic, less motivated, learn slower, make poorer decisions, have lower confidence and self-esteem, are more prone to mental illnesses, including depression, and are slower to bounce back from setbacks—and these are only some of the symptoms of unhappiness.

No wonder unhappy people are exhausted.

Is It Time For A Change?

Change isn't always easy. It takes a lot of planning, effort and preparation. But the results are worth it. A well-planned change brings new beginnings, fresh experiences and a job that fulfils and energizes your life.

Despite all the positive benefits that a fresh start can bring, you may well find that until the pain of remaining the same hurts more than the effort required to change, it can be hard to get motivated.

Using your knowledge and clarity about what's causing your job blues will help you identify possible solutions, and tap into the powerful energy of intention to create positive changes.

The Positivity of Negativity

Setbacks can sometimes be opportunities in disguise. As you look back, times which seemed like low points can, with hindsight, prove to be the most life-changing and meaningful experiences. If your job is draining you this can prove challenging. It is hard to feel optimistic when you are depleted.

However, Viktor Frankl, an Austrian psychiatrist who survived the horrors of the Nazi death camps, believes that it's not the situation which defines and controls us but our attitudes and reactions.

Somehow, he urges us, we must endeavor to look for meaning and purpose in situations that cause us to suffer. If after everything Viktor Frankl went though he can find something positive in the most horrific of situations, it's something you can do too.

The challenge, if you're up for it, is to constantly strive to look for the silver linings in stormy weather. For example, the fact that you are unhappy at work is a silver lining in disguise—it's the motivating force you need to make a change!

These same principles apply whether you're a stay-at-home-mum contemplating a return to work, or if you have been out of work for some time. By recalling the times you've been unhappy you'll gain greater clarity about what you need to feel happy at work. And vice versa.

Jasmine, a clinical psychologist once told me, "The job's just not me. I need a new one but I don't know what I want." By listing the things she didn't like, as well as the things she enjoyed in both her current and previous roles, she was better able to identify the things which were important to her. Building this list of criteria for job satisfaction helped her narrow where to begin her search.

Cultivating a Liberating Attitude

Thinking optimistically and living in constant gratitude for what you do have versus over-focusing on what you don't have increases confidence, hope, feelings of satisfaction and happiness—all necessary preparatory ingredients for positive transitions.

It is no coincidence that the successful people in life see the cup half full and look for ways to add more to people's lives, rather than demand or expect others top them up.

Successful, liberated people are also smart—they know how to accept the things they can't change and take control of the things they can.

Like any skill, cultivating a liberated attitude is something anyone can learn.

"There will come a time when you believe everything is finished that will be the beginning" ~ *Louis L'Amour, Author*

Client Success Story: From Despair to Gratitude

Diana, hated her job so much the strain was beginning to take a toll. When she started her job as a designer for a large international company she thought it was great.

But the workload was excruciating—she soon found that she was doing a job that previously needed three people. She quickly felt overloaded and drained of energy.

The pressure was getting to her and she talked of being the sickest she had ever been in her life. She shared her feelings of frustration and admitted that she spent most of her day complaining about the things she didn't like about her job with her colleagues.

When she wasn't at work she moaned to her friends and to her partner. She wished she could say, 'I quit' but couldn't afford to financially. Diana felt trapped.

Diana began to wonder if her illness was a direct result of feeling at 'dis-ease' with her job and sought career counselling to help her work out a cure.

I asked her how—given that she was not able to resign in the short term—she felt she could make her current work situation more bearable, even enjoyable.

She found generating ideas hard and couldn't think of any possible solutions. I encouraged her to buy a journal and write down all the things about her current job she was grateful for. This threw her a bit!

After a particularly bad day she drew up her list which included: she was employed and had a steady wage; earned overtime for extra hours; worked close to where she lived; had access to great products and services; had six weeks paid leave; and that she liaised with international buyers and people at the top of their field that she could learn from.

After completing this list Diana said she felt immediately *"lighter"* and better about her job. She began to see what a vicious self-fulfilling cycle her negative attitude to work was having and made a conscious decision to stop talking about what she didn't like.

She vowed to only speak in positive terms or not at all. As she began to feel happier and more energized Diana found it easier to see potential solutions to her career rut.

She put forward a proposal to redefine her job and responsibilities. This wasn't accepted by her boss, but rather than become negative and resentful Diana looked for the silver lining.

She felt that by not getting what she wanted she was being prompted to get clear about what she did want long term and to start preparing for the time when she would leave.

She set some goals and developed an action plan to bring more passion into both her private and personal life. Knowing that she was beginning to take some positive steps to move the detrimental out of her life and make room for the positive, and choosing to see obstacles as learning experiences, made her remaining time less painful.

One year later she set up her own design company.

"I truly believe that absent the victim mentality, everyone—regardless of background, education, or ability—can carve out a good path for themselves in this tumultuous workplace."
~ *Richard Bolles, Author*

Action Task! Your Gratitudes

What's right about your career and life right now? Jot down some things that come to mind. Create a gratitude section in your passion journal and add to it regularly.

Client Success Story: From Problems To Solutions

Jeremy was feeling very frustrated in his job and talked constantly about all the things that weren't going well. Focusing on problems made him feel more and more angry and frustrated.

His irritability and despondency began to take a negative toll on his self-esteem and confidence and infected his relationships with his boss and co-workers.

It was hard to contain his feelings to work, and before long his frustrations began to take a toll on his marriage. To shift him from a problems focus to a solutions focus, he wrote down the things that frustrated him and looked for the silver linings and opportunities for personal development that these things created.

A summary of these are below. He created a list of 'action items' to help him prepare for and leverage off any opportunities, including making a time to speak to HR and his manager with the aim of creating development opportunities within his workplace. His preparation, including becoming more comfortable asking for his needs to be met, paid off and he was offered a secondment into a new division.

Frustration: My skills are unappreciated

Opportunity: I am learning that I need to be more comfortable 'blowing my own trumpet' and telling people what I have achieved

Frustration: All they do is talk about things—nothing gets done

Opportunity: I have the opportunity to listen, utilize and learn from people who have skills I want to develop

Frustration: Recognition is just related to money billed

Opportunity: I need to take responsibility for communicating my own career drivers and suggesting some other ways that I would like to be rewarded for my efforts

Frustration: My boss is a bully

Opportunity: I am learning how to stand up for myself and not be intimidated by 'challenging' personalities. Knowledge is power and I seek help from people who know how to deal with these issues

Frustration: I'm bored

Opportunity: The lack of challenge is motivating me to feel the fear and do it anyway—i.e., leave and find a new job that stretches me

Action Task! Your Silver Linings

Create your own record of possible silver linings and notice how your energy shifts and how you begin to feel as you move from focusing on problems to looking for solutions. Continue the exercise in your passion journal whenever you feel frustrated or discouraged.

The Courage to Define What You Want

It may feel easier to go for the comfortable option when thinking about a career change. You may feel you lack energy, or confidence, to set your sights higher. Or you may feel you face very real barriers to employment, and lack the drive and self-belief to overcome setbacks.

In all my years of career counselling the biggest barrier I've found when working with clients is helping them believe they can manifest their dreams.

Fear of disappointment and even of success often underlies many peoples' reluctance to define what they want. As one of my clients said, "If I tell you my dream I might realize I can't achieve it. Then not only will I have failed but I'll have lost my dream."

Failure to set and follow through on career goals is one of the biggest reasons that only 10% of people are visibly pursuing their passion, and why well over 63% of people are dissatisfied with their work.

Using insights gained from this chapter and the exercises in the following chapters will help you have the courage to define what you want and develop the mindset and skills to achieve it.

Affirm what you want!

Once you are clear about the forces that drive your decisions, finding a job that you like is easier. It won't happen overnight but it will happen! But first you need to get clear about what your perfect job would look like.

Action Task! Your Criteria For Job Satisfaction

In your passion journal head up a page: "Criteria for Job Satisfaction." Re-frame any of the negative statements you identified in the dissatisfaction quiz at the beginning of this chapter into positive statements about what you *do* want.

You may also want to include a brief statement about why it is important to you. For example, if you wrote: "I get no feedback," write something like, "I want to receive feedback on a regular basis. This is important to me because I want to feel valued and to know that what I have done is appreciated."

Add to this list all the things about your current job or previous jobs that you've enjoyed. Don't worry if you don't have many things on your list. This is only the beginning and as you work through some of the exercises in the rest of the series you will gain more ideas about all the ingredients that make a job satisfying to you.

From Strain To Gain

When I first decided on a career as a recruitment consultant I thought it would be a great opportunity to help people find jobs they enjoyed and to use my coaching skills.

I didn't realize that the major part of the job was sales and business development. The seeds of dissatisfaction festered as I realized that I was not using the skills that I enjoyed.

In addition, the things that were really important to me, such as the value I placed on helping people, were compromised. It was a sales culture where the commission earned by putting people into jobs or a workplace, that I knew wasn't a good fit, was more important than helping people find the *right* job.

For a long time I tried to ignore my unhappiness. Finding another job seemed like too much work and secretly I couldn't help but wonder if maybe I expected too much from my job. Shouldn't I be grateful to have an income? My self-esteem plummeted and I felt too frightened to look for another job— what if nobody else wanted me?

Before long my growing 'dis-ease' with my job bubbled out into painful blisters. I was quickly diagnosed with shingles.

Until I'd experienced what it was like not to do what I enjoyed I didn't realize how important these things were to me. I started to look for ways to do more of what I wanted and less of what I didn't. When the opportunity came to move into the career management team I leapt at the chance. I enjoyed it but I still didn't get to do what I really wanted—hands on coaching.

Several years later, with my eye to the future, I left the company altogether and aligned myself with a role much more in tune with my soul and my longer-term goals.

Then later still I left the security of that salaried job and embraced the freedom of self-employment and owning my own business. I was a single mum—the sole breadwinner—with a mortgage. There was no safety net other than the preparation I'd done and the belief and knowledge that I had saleable skills which were in demand. I've never looked back.

Saying Hello And Goodbye

Some of the things I said hello to when I made a move were increased freedom, autonomy and earnings. I said goodbye to being controlled, and having a cap on my salary.

While there were trade-offs, such as no longer having paid annual leave and statutory holidays, the benefits, including the ability to work from home and the flexibility to care for my daughter—especially during her school holidays—more than compensated for any losses.

Action Task! Hello-Goodbye

Say hello to your preferred future and goodbye to the past by creating your own hello-goodbye list in your passion journal. Remember to include the benefits you'll gain by releasing what no longer serves you. Add to this list as you gain more insights from the exercises in the following chapter:

Surf The Net

Listen to my interview on Radio New Zealand, and hear more about being happy at work. Click here:

http://worklifesolutions.nz/media/tv-radio-and-youtube/

"Change is the end result of all true learning. Change involves three things: First, a dissatisfaction with self—a felt void or need; second, a decision to change—to fill the void or need; and third, a conscious dedication to the process of growth and change—the willful act of making the change; Doing Something."
~ Dr Phil

Dissatisfaction Quiz

Before you find the cure to your job blues you first need to get clear about what's causing the problem. The following Dissatisfaction Quiz will help.

Perhaps you can identify with some of the common causes of dissatisfaction below.

In your journal record (or highlight in your eBook!) the statements below that are true for you.

You may find that this is a useful starting point in identifying what needs to change in order to be happy at work. Your answers can also highlight which parts or books in the series will be most helpful to you.

1. You don't know what your skills are or what you're good at

2. Lack of recognition—people don't value you and what you do

3. You're bored and your job lacks challenge—you can't see any opportunity for growth or advancement

4. The culture is very negative

5. You don't get on with your co-workers

6. You feel stuck and can't see a way to make any improvements

7. You keep getting looked over for promotion

8. You don't know what makes you happy

9. You're not doing the things that really matter to you

10. The job doesn't meet your values

11. Your life feels out of balance

12. The workload is too heavy

13. Your job pays the bills but your passions are left as a hobby

14. You have a growing sense—vague though it might be—that you could improve the quality of your life

15. You have very little autonomy and control over your work

16. Your role or organization isn't spiritually aligned to the things you believe in

17. Office politics get you down

18. Your job and/or work environment is not fun

19. People don't have pride in their work, and poor performance is often ignored

20. Your wages are too low

21. The organization is too bureaucratic—policies and procedures slow everything down

22. You're not using the skills you enjoy

23. You feel 'boxed' in and don't know how to get into something different

24. You don't know what you want to do

25. Only the bosses' ideas are listened to

26. Your job lacks security

27. Very little about the job interests you

28. You have lost your confidence and your self-esteem is low

29. You're not achieving your potential

30. You park the 'real you' at the door—the robotic you goes to work

31. Personal issues are impacting on your enjoyment of work—these issues affect your focus, and motivation, etc.

32. The work environment isn't very attractive

33. Lack of training and support makes it difficult to do your job well

34. People are bullied and/or not treated with respect

35. Your role lacks meaning and purpose—you don't feel that what you contribute makes a difference

Scoring:

0-6 Congratulations! Nothing really seems to be getting you down. Perhaps you're just looking for a new challenge. Read on for tips and strategies to help you move in a new direction.

6-20 if you answered "yes" to 6 or more of these statements you are moderately dissatisfied with the way things are going in your life. Develop specific actions for identifying and incorporating passion into your life.

21-35 You are suffering from severe dissatisfaction. You really do deserve to pursue a more satisfying alternative. Take immediate steps now to create positive changes in your work and life. In addition to applying the strategies in this book you may wish to solicit the support of a professional.

What You've Learned So Far

- The job-blues can be a powerful motivating force for change. By putting the spotlight on what you don't want, the sources of your unhappiness can point you in the direction of your heart's desire.

- Looking for the silver linings can help you transform a crisis into an opportunity.

- The body barometer never lies. Feelings of tiredness and activities that drain you are signs that you are settling for less. Feelings of depression, boredom and lifelessness are signs from your intuition that you are ignoring your passion. Take time to reprioritize your life and focus on what gives you energy and happiness, and start letting go of everything that drains you.

- Happiness isn't something that just happens—it's something we actively participate in creating. There's no better place to start than training your mind, and shaping your attitude—even when life turns to lumpy custard you'll still manage to find something to be grateful for.

- Take control—feeling helpless, accepting the unacceptable, and procrastinating about taking action can lead to feelings of depression, hopelessness and quickly erode your confidence. Taking action will quickly help to get rid of the job blues.

- Your mind has the power to influence your reality. As you begin to envision your preferred future, notice how your dreams and intentions begin to not only influence your attitudes and actions, but how it will reach and influence the circumstances of your life. All things are created twice—first mentally and then physically.

- The desire for a better life and maintaining a positive expectancy will give you the motivational kick-start you need to break out of your rut and pursue the happiness you deserve.

What's Next?

In the next chapter we're going to look at why it's a great time to be a mid-lifer and look at ways to reframe any mistaken beliefs you, or those you want to work for, may have about being at your age and stage.

"To the poor old mid-life worker, it can seem like nothing is possible. The reality is nothing could be further from the truth. People are changing jobs and starting new lives continually."
~ *Fitzsimons and Beckford, Authors*

THE GIFT OF LONGEVITY

It is a great time for mid-lifers to make the leap to a new career, but for some people this means reframing their expectations of employment.

Embracing the new world of work, where it seems likely that many people will continue to work in paid employment into their late 60s, 70s and beyond, means a mindset change for not just employers but also, more importantly, for individuals themselves.

Many countries and organizations are facing a critical skills shortage as fewer and fewer younger people enter the workforce and mature workers continue to opt out of mainstream employment.

Among these messages of impending disaster at a conference I attended in Italy it was refreshing to hear delegates from France, Italy and Australia reframe the issues from a problem to an opportunity and to speak about positive ageing and the "gift of longevity."

But so many of the more 'mature' clients I coach still feel their age is a problem. They worry that they are too old to change careers, and despair they have left it too late to change.

"My life has been a life of regret," one of my clients said. At the ripe young age of 45 he couldn't see much hope of improving his situation.

Similarly Mike a professional man in his late 50s told me he was too old to change career. He also worried that employers would feel the same way. After reading this book and some follow up coaching he changed his mindset and opportunities flooded his way.

He's now working in a role that his friends say looks like it was tailor-made just for him.

"Some really great news—I've just heard I got the job I went after. Can hardly believe it after trying to find a way into this area of work for a long time. For me it's confirmation of the importance and power of managing my thought processes," he wrote.

Worryingly it's not just older workers that have pessimistic job expectations. "Don't you do what you love when you retire?" one 25-year-old client asked me. I was stunned. "Where did you learn that?" I asked. "It's what my mother told me," she confessed.

"Mid-life is a time to reinvent ourselves and make new choices based on what we truly want. The challenge is to look at the changing energy with anticipation. We can throw away the roles that do not serve and open to ones that contain more freedom to be ourselves."
~*Barbara Biziou, Author*

Are You Stuck In The Dark Ages?

Authors of *You Don't Make a Big Leap Without a Gulp: Having the Courage to Change Careers and Live Again*, Mike Fitzsimons and Nigel Beckford, suggest that many people are trapped in a Depression-era mind-set, thinking, "I'm lucky to have a job," or "I'll sit it out until I retire."

An article in *Time Magazine* also confirmed the reality that many mature workers have been conditioned to expect less from the world of work. As a result they often have negative views or expectations about the wealth of opportunity that now exists.

The reality is that there's a huge amount of opportunity out there for people wanting more from their working lives than to grit their teeth and bear it. Or for those who want to gain greater financial security than the $288 superannuation per week currently on offer from the New Zealand Government. As Eleanor Roosevelt once said, "The future belongs to those who believe in the beauty of their dreams."

Breaking Free

The greatest challenge we mid-lifers have is to actively break free from narrow views of what is possible and embrace a sense of adventure.

To gain the courage to change careers and the skills to hunt for jobs successfully requires the ability and willingness to challenge assumptions.

Changing careers mid-life also requires a healthy dose of inspiration, a commitment to careful planning and the willingness to take calculated risks.

Fitzsimons and Beckford urge middle-aged workers to rekindle a sense of adventure and embrace the wealth of opportunity that exists now for mature people in the workforce.

Their research suggests that people spend lots of time looking after their teeth and monitoring their cholesterol levels, but neglect to spend time having regular career checks.

Does this sound like you? If so, where and how do you start planning your mid-life career transition?

Embracing the New World of Possibilities

The Association of Career Professionals International says that adopting a creative and lateral approach to career and work choices is the key to embracing the new world of possibilities.

They urge vocational guidance practitioners to encourage clients to be imaginative when thinking about ways to combine skills, talents and interests to secure paid employment.

But being creative isn't the way many mid-lifers have been encouraged to think about careers! You may have experienced the old narrow model of career decision-making where you were told what you could do. For example, women were told their choices were severely limited to roles such as nursing, teaching, typing or being a wife.

Or perhaps you've been conditioned to think a job has to be just one thing, and that this one thing, is something you only do from an office, from 9-5 or longer.

Thankfully for people today there are almost unlimited career choices, and various ways to bundle the work week.

Helping people like you think laterally and creatively about careers is my strength and my passion! But first let's get you started thinking positively about your life stage.

The Changing World Of Work

Over the last 10 years we have seen unprecedented change. Globalization and technological revolutions such as the Internet and mobile devices have made it so much easier for companies and individuals to generate income anywhere, anytime.

This has led to many benefits, including a wider variety of goods and services, and a diversity of employment scenarios. Now you have an increased ability to generate income from the comfort of your own home, and greater opportunities to live and work overseas.

Len, aged 54, runs a thriving recruitment business from the beautiful serenity of his lifestyle property. Sally lives on a neighboring property, using Skype, email and her phone, is able to manage her very successful mortgage company.

And you don't have to be self-employed to benefit from technological and global advancements. Numerous businesses offer flexible working arrangements to attract and retain staff.

The increased level of commercial and competitive pressures has also meant that companies, and their employees, need to constantly re-invent themselves to keep up. This is great news for mid-lifers wanting to make a positive change.

A List Of Changes Impacting Work

The list below highlights how some of these changes have impacted on work and careers. Add to this list any changes that you or those close to you have personally experienced or know of.

The Changing World of Work Table

The list below highlights how some of these changes have impacted on work and careers. Add to this list any changes that you or those close to you have personally experienced or know of.

The Past	Now
A job for life	Multiple jobs
Predictable career path	Varied career paths
Apprenticeships	Learn off the job/Pay your own training
Loyalty to one organization	Loyalty to self
Narrowly defined role	Multi-tasking/Project-based work
Managers	Leaders
Work with hands	Work with head/Knowledge workers
Protected economy	Global economy/competition
Limited choices/opportunities	Unlimited choices/opportunities

Gender-specific roles	Gender-neutral roles
Limited technology	Constantly changing technology
IQ—intellectual intelligence	EQ—emotional intelligence
Organizational hierarchies	Flat structures
Full-time employment	Contract, part-time and portfolio work
Employee	Contractor
Stable workforce	High turnover of employees
Labor surplus	Labor shortage (changing demographics)
One job (9-5)	Portfolio work/Job combo
Job matching	Job creation/Job sculpting
Tied to a location	Independent of location
Bricks and mortar	Virtual Office

Can you think of any other changes impacting how we live and work? What new opportunities might any shifts in the world of work create for you?

Action Tasks! Aging Positively

If you're like Mike and feel your age is against you it's time to get a mindset shift. There are numerous ways to maintain a positive approach to increasing age. Here are just a few examples:

1. **Start collecting evidence of positive ageing.** Compile an inspirational mid-life file and add clippings, photos, quotes and 'case studies' of people who have made it big, or are happy at work, in their twilight years. Look for your role models.
Gather at least 10 examples of successful people in your age group and above. You'll see a few of my favorite examples in the pages which follow.

2. **Create an image board or journal.** Paste inspirational quotes, pictures and clippings which celebrate maturity in the workforce and life. Motivate yourself by adding to it and looking at it regularly.

3. **Turn age into an asset.** Don't be disheartened by people who think your age is against you. Write down a list of the benefits of hiring a mature worker. Widen your awareness of the positives by asking others to add their views. Armed with your own self-belief and a few powerful strategies to market yourself, you'll be unstoppable.

4. **Network with other like-minded people.** Talk to other mature job seekers, check helpful websites, and network with organizations that provide tips and examples to help you succeed and stay positive.

5. **Get career fit.** Learn a new skill or get up to date with new technology that will help you gain the job you want. You're never too old to learn, and you may even discover a new talent.

6. **Rekindle a sense of adventure.** Re-awaken dormant creative skills and adopt a playful approach to life. Take on some FTEs—first time experiences. Can you think of anything you'd love to try? Like Carla Coulson, who in her

40's gave photography a go, found a new passion and has now made it a rewarding career.

7. **Challenge your assumptions.** Divide a page into half. List any negative assumptions you might have about your age and on the other side write some counter statements. Here's an example to get you started:

Negative Assumptions

Employers prefer younger workers

Affirming Counter Statements

Demographic research shows that companies are going to need to recruit from a more mature labor pool

"There is no substitute for bravery, creative thinking and imagination if you want a rewarding career."
~ *Peter Biggs, Former CEO of Creative New Zealand*

Plenty Of Time To Make It Big

The encouraging news, according to some experts, is that life begins in the late 40's. Evidence suggests that many people don't reach their potential until well into their 50s and 60s.

American grandfather of motivational books, Napoleon Hill, whose best-selling book, *Think and Grow Rich*, was published for the first time in 1937, discovered from an analysis of more than 25,000 people that those who succeed seldom do before the age of 40, and usually do not strike their real pace until well beyond their 50's.

This data should be encouraging for those who 'fail to arrive' before 50 and offers compelling evidence that people should approach the mid-years with hope and anticipation!

It's Never Too Late

Here are just a few people who have achieved success in their later years:

1. Author Helen Hoover Santmyer was 88-years-young when her book *And Ladies of the Club* was published. It stayed on the New York Times Best-sellers list for eight months. It was her first novel in 50 years.

2. A failure at 65, Colonel Sanders was world-famous and wealthy at 80. His father was a miner and his mother worked in a shirt factory. Harland Sanders had to give up school in the sixth grade because he was so poor.

   He eventually opened a small home-town restaurant in the Kentucky hills. All looked well until the highway was rerouted and he lost everything. He was 65 at the time and faced with a future barely surviving on social security, his motivation to try again kicked in.

   "My government is going to give me a hundred and five dollars so I can eke out an existence. Surely there is something I can do for myself and other people."

   Tapping into powerfully creative questions like this unlocked the key to what would be his major success—his mother's secret chicken recipe.

   Turned down by numerous restaurants at the time he turned potential failure into another inspired idea—franchises. It was an instantaneous hit, and the rest is history!

3. Fifty-five-year-old Rhonda Byrne's life was at an all-time low. Twice divorced, her father had just died and her career was in crisis.

That was until, acting on an inspired thought, she created the DVD The Secret and later produced a book, both of which went on to becoming some of the biggest-selling self-help resources of all time.

At the heart of Rhonda's inspirational series of products and resources is the law of attraction.

"Everything in your life is attracted to you by what you are thinking," Rhonda says. "You are like a human transmission tower, transmitting a frequency with your thoughts. **If you want to change anything in your life, change the frequency by changing your thoughts**."

Action Questions: How Can You Think Positive?

Take a leaf from Rhonda's secret to success and change any stinkin' thinkin' that may be lingering. Answering the following questions may help:

1. What results are you currently experiencing that you would like to change?

2. What thoughts would you need to change?

3. What thoughts would remain the same?

4. What things have supported you in maintaining a positive state of mind in the past? How could they be helpful now?

5. Can you think of some other strategies to help you keep your mind on what you want and off what you don't want?

"We all have big changes in our lives that are more or less a second chance."
*~ **Harrison Ford, Actor***

Client Success Story: From Unemployed to Franchise Manager

Aged 48, Ngaire returned to New Zealand after running a business in outback Australia. Things had not gone well after an economic downturn in the rural economy and she walked away from her business. Ngaire tried her hand at a few other things but realized there were few prospects for her in Australia so came home.

She returned penniless and alone with no work prospects. She was unsure if her skills were suitable for more modern careers, and initially thought about learning computer skills.

However, a friend encouraged her to read this book and work through a career coaching process. This helped her recognize and value her experience and realize how her current skills could transfer into other jobs.

Ngaire had always walked easily into work, because she had lived in a town where everyone knew her and there was plenty of work.

After learning how to value and communicate her transferable skills and experience she re-wrote her CV, and was successful in getting a job as a shop manager for a national food franchise. Her new employer valued her prior experience, maturity and management potential.

Ngaire achieved great success in her role and turned around many problem stores. She was quickly promoted and given more responsibility. Her pay packet received a nice boost too!

It takes courage and strength of character to leave a situation and start over again. Ngaire's secret to success was drive, determination and a solid work ethic.

Initially despondent and fearful, she is now happy, confident and not worried about her future. Ngaire realizes that there are more opportunities out there and that she has the power to create her own luck and seize opportunities that come her way.

Her employer, had the foresight to take on a mature person, and together they benefit in ways they hadn't foreseen.

Robert Kiyosaki, multi-millionaire entrepreneur and author, is right when he says, "There is no one in your way except you and your doubts about you. It is easy to stay the same. It is not easy to change. Most people choose to stay the same all their lives. If you take on your self-doubt and your laziness you will find the door to your freedom."

A Time Of Renewal

You are as old as you choose to feel. I know many people in their 70's and 80's who are still leading active work lives and enjoying a more healthier existence as a result.

"If you retire you expire," says 88-year-old Boyd Klap who vows never to stop contributing.

Check out this video (http://https://vimeo.com/122707475) and watch the value of being mutually inspired and inspiring, and of maintaining a spirit of curiosity through and beyond your middle ages. You'll see Mandy Scott-Mackie who had just embarked on a mid-life career adventure in outback Australia and Boyd Klap who tried retiring many times and got bored!

Action Task! Visualise Your Future

For some, getting older can herald more opportunities. While for others, especially those without a nest egg, or a working partner to fall back on, seeking help to reinvent their lives and careers is critical.

Whatever situation you find yourself in, going with the flow and waiting for life to 'happen' won't provide the emotional and financial security that we baby boomers seek. **Actively plan for your preferred future, because that's where you're going to be spending the rest of your life.**

The following sensory visualization exercise will not only help you clarify your preferred future, but it will also help you power up your sub-conscious mind:

1) Draw a time line and put yourself on it.

Project yourself toward your preferred future—10, 15, or 20 years from now. How old will you be? Note this down. Now create your ideal life in your mind's eye. Engage all your senses and record your responses to the following questions (try visually displaying your responses on an image or dream board).

What sights are around you? Are you surrounded by people who love you or enjoying the solitude of nature? Are you living overseas in an elegant, romantic, calm environment or are you somewhere more high energy, bustling and commercial? What colors and things surround you? What do you see?

What can you hear—the peacefulness of the country, cries of acclaim for something you have done, laughter, live music, bird song or something else?

What smells fill the air? The smell of your partner's cologne or perfume as you work from home? The sweet, aromatic smell of freshly picked grapes from your vineyard? What does your preferred future smell like to you?

How does your preferred future feel? Is it like the warm, smooth earth surrounding the lifestyle home where you live and work? The silky coats of the horses you train? The fine linen of your business suit or the smooth denim of your jeans as your turn up to deliver a seminar? Notice all the textures that surround you.

How does your ideal life taste? Are you enjoying the foods from your organic garden? Fine cuisine on your overseas travels? Amazing meals out dining with clients as you travel the world? Or something else

By visualizing your preferred future and engaging your senses you have taken the first step in making your dreams your reality.

2) What's stopping you from living your dream now?

Note these things down, but resist the feeling of being stuck by actively willing your mind to create solutions. Ask generative questions like: How can I make my dream real? Where can I get help? How can I make a change?

Look back along your time line and think about all the steps you would have to do to make things happen.

Who would you need to talk to? What information would you need to know? What finance would you need to acquire? How can you acquire it? What training or new skills would you need?

3) On your time line begin to map out the stepping stones to your success and do something every day, no matter how small, to move you closer to your dream.

Don't worry if you don't have all the answers. This is only the beginning of your career adventure. The rest of the exercises in this book will help you fill in any gaps.

Preparing For Success

There is only one security in this life—the ability to manage change.

Below are a few strategies to help you prepare for a successful change:

1.) Increase your self-awareness. "Pause for a cup of tea, David Lange, former Prime Minister of New Zealand once said, when people were rushing prematurely into critical decision-making that affected the country's future. Increase your self-awareness. Take time out to clarify what it is that you really want—and why.
How can we have a knowledge economy if we lack self-knowledge? Listen to my interview on Radio New Zealand about this and other issues related to changing careers: http://www.worklifesolutions.co.nz/wp-content/uploads/2012/05/01-Radio-New-Zealand-Interview-2004-48kbps-1.mp3

2.) Play. Approach the career planning process with an adventurous, curious spirit. In the early stages remind yourself that you are exploring. Deciding can come later. Nurture and encourage curiosity and allow yourself to dream. Ask yourself, "what if…"

It's also interesting to note the increasing emphasis being given to adults now to embrace their inner, fearless child. Tap into the 'kidult' trend to help with modern day challenges, advocate a range of experts, and work towards an idealized world, free of restraint. You may just surprise yourself.

3.) Spend time researching your options and generating alternative possibilities. **Actively challenge any assumptions that may be holding you back.**

4.) Affirm the positive. Keep your mind on what you do want and off what you don't. Your truest beliefs become your thoughts, your deepest thoughts become your words, your spoken and unspoken words become your actions, your concrete actions become your habits, your conscious and unconscious habits become your values and your values become your destiny.

5.) Get inspired! Surround yourself with all the things that give you joy. Sidestep the things that give you stress and look after your health so you have energy to make changes.

6.) Plan for success and set yourself free. Know when it's time to stop thinking about changing and time to take concrete steps toward your preferred future.

Work through the exercises in this book and buddy up with someone who believes in the beauty of your dreams and can help you stay on track.

Client Success Story: From IT Account Manager to Travel Agent

Bill Kwan's wake-up call happened in his 40s, when increasing stress levels made a career move not just a nice thing to do, but a necessity. As his wife said, "If you don't leave now it will kill you."

Some people may have taken the easier option by taking stress leave or an extended holiday, but Bill chose to take a career leap and shift from a senior account management role with an international IT company to work in an area that had always interested him—travel.

He initially worked as a travel consultant for a local travel agency. However, changing careers did come at a price.

"I didn't just take a salary drop—it was a salary plummet," he says. However, **what he sacrificed in salary was made up for in personal fulfilment**. "I gained more time to spend with my wife and daughter, play golf and work in an area that I love."

"Follow your desire, but make sure you plan for success," Bill says.

Bill already had his eye on his longer-term goal when he accepted the junior role as travel agent. Two years after making his first move he has just purchased his own agency.

> "Often people try to live their lives backwards: they try to have more things, or more money, in order to do more of what they want so they will be happier. The way it actually works is the reverse. You must first be who you really are, then do what you really need to do, in order to have what you want."
> ~ *Margaret Young, Author*

What You've Learned So Far

- Times have changed and age is now on the side for the baby boomer generation as skills shortages begin to bite and demographic shifts mean there are fewer younger people in the labor force.

- Economic, demographic, social and technological changes have altered the career landscape. There is a huge amount of opportunity for people wanting to reinvent their working lives.

- The greatest challenge for mid-lifers is the willingness to embrace a sense of adventure and to think laterally and creatively about career possibilities.

- It's never too late too make it big—planning, passion, courage and positive views about ageing are important catalysts to successful change.

- Nearly anything is possible—the mid-years are a wonderful time of renewal.

- Increasing your self-awareness, being inspired, dreaming about your preferred future and having a compelling vision are important parts of the change process.

What's Next?

Taking care of yourself is another important, but often neglected, part of making a successful career change. Making changes, even positive ones, can send the stress levels soaring.

You may have been so unhappy in your previous role that you are already stressed out. Or perhaps the stress of being out of work for so long is beginning to take a toll.

The following chapter will help you get your groove back. Stress less and build greater stress resilience through the change process by working through the exercises which follow.

STRESS LESS

Perhaps you've been feeling stressed before you downloaded this book. Have you been unhappy at work for so long that some of the symptoms of stress, such as feelings of depression, anxiety or even anger, are really entrenched.

Or is the idea of making a change causing you to feel anxious? Whatever your current situation there is no doubt that managing stress is a key component of making effective career decisions.

Stress is something we all feel everyday. It isn't something that only happens when we're under particular pressure. Some mild stress is good for you. It gives you a feeling of excitement and makes you want to strive to do better. It reminds you that you're alive, and it can help you thrive.

But too much stress can do the opposite. Stress overload can make you feel overwhelmed and empty, devoid of enthusiasm; or worse, of a will to live.

Negative thoughts and feelings are a classic sign of too much stress. It's hard to feel hopeful about the future when you are feeling down, overwhelmed or anxious.

So it's not surprising that it can be hard to believe in yourself, or to remember the things that make you happy. More often than not, during times of strain your self-esteem and confidence can take an awful hit.

Biologically we're incapable of sustaining prolonged levels of stress, no matter how great our will. If you don't address your stress, your body's adaptive resources can become exhausted— making you sick. Too much stress can give you chronic headaches, affect your blood pressure, contribute to depression and cause ulcers and heart disease.

Thankfully there are simple but powerful strategies at hand to help you avoid too much 'bad' stress, so you don't become ill, anxious or depressed during the change process.

And who knows, maybe once you have your stress levels back in check, or have found ways to proactively remove the sources of stress in either your work or private life, you may end up falling back in love with a job that you'd come to hate.

Heed The Early Warning Signs

According to a definition from The New Zealand Department of Occupational Safety and Health (OSH), stress is a reaction to the excess pressures you face in your life, and arises when you feel you can't cope.

This feeling of not being able to cope is an important point I will come back to, but one of the key things to remember is that worrying about not coping, even if it is not actively voiced, triggers the promotion of stress messages in your brain.

You may be so busy trying to juggle everything that you are unaware of how much strain you are under. Like Roger, who hates his career so much he says he hates his life. Or Jan, who can't relax, and is so busy being busy that she can't remember the last time she felt real joy.

The Biology Of Stress

When your life lacks balance this leads to a state of brain chemical imbalance known as—OVER STRESS. These negative brain messages then flow to other organs in your body sending them into overdrive and a high state of alert.

People who are overstressed complain of being tired but unable to fall asleep or enjoy a restful night's sleep. They have plagues of aches and pains, lack of energy, and can't remember what makes them feel truly happy. They feel depressed, anxious, tearful, snappy and irritable or just unable to cope with life.

Many people soldier on ignoring the signs their body is giving them. Some live to tell their stories and the lessons they learnt. As I've already said, I was so stressed and unhappy at work I got shingles. Others aren't so 'lucky.' One of my colleagues suffered a heart attack and later died.

Stress is an invisible killer, and the underlying cause of mental illness, depression and suicide. It's that serious—no wonder the onus on employers to help employees manage stress has been written into health and safety legislation.

But don't rely on anyone else to be proactive about your well-being.

Listen To Your Body Barometer

The key to managing stress successfully is to heed the early warning signs. By nipping your stressors in the bud before they go to seed, you will avoid wreaking havoc with your body, mind and spirit.

You'll also avoid derailing your career and damaging your relationships. Increasing your coping skills can also be a wonder cure for dissatisfaction with your work, or your life.

"He who is of a calm and happy nature will hardly feel the pressure of age."
~ **Plato**

Your Body Barometer Test

How Stressed Are You?

Take the following body barometer test by taking note of any symptoms you're currently experiencing.

Physical Signs of Stress

- Increased heart rate/Pounding heart
- Sweaty palms
- Elevated blood pressure
- Tightness of the chest, neck, jaw and back muscles
- Headaches
- Diarrhea/Constipation
- Unable to pass urine or incontinence
- Trembling/Twitching
- Stuttering and other speech difficulties
- Nausea/Vomiting
- Sleep disturbances
- Fatigue
- Being easily startled
- Shallow, rapid breathing
- Dryness of mouth or throat

- Cold hands
- Susceptibility to minor illnesses
- Itching
- Chronic pain

Emotional Signs of Stress

- Tearful
- Impatience
- Frightened
- Moody
- Highs and lows
- Feeling of loss
- Depressed
- Anger
- Irritated
- Short-tempered
- Grief

Cognitive/Perceptual/Thinking Signs

- Forgetfulness
- Preoccupation
- Errors in judging distance/space
- Reduced creativity/creative thinking

- Lack of concentration

- Diminished productivity

- Lack of attention to detail

- Orientation to the past

- Diminished reaction time

- Clumsiness

- Disorganization of thought

- Negative self-esteem

- Negative self-statements

- Diminished sense of meaning in life

- Lack of control/Need for too much control

- Negative evaluation of experiences

- Negative thinking

- Pessimism

Behavioural Signs of Stress

- Carelessness/Accident prone

- Under-eating/Over-eating

- Aggressiveness/Fighting/Hostility

- Increased smoking/Starting smoking

- Withdrawal

- Argumentative

- Increased alcohol or drug use

- Listlessness

- Nervous laughter

- Compulsive behavior

- Impatience/Agitation

Take a look at the following stress-busting tips and create your own stress management plan at the end of this chapter. Starting from a positive, healthy foundation will help you make changes in your career and life successfully.

"Whether or not a person experiences stress at work depends upon the person's perception of what is going on and the person's coping skills. It is not the circumstance, it is your REACTION to it that counts."
~ Dr Al Siebert, Author

Action Tasks! Stress-Busting and Building Resilience

1) Identify what's stressing you out—stress is cumulative, and if it's prolonged, or we have too much on the go at once, our normal coping skills can be diminished.

Making a list of all the things that are worrying you or that stress you out, and then trying to work out solutions, is an effective way to get some control over your stress levels. Think possibilities not actualities to unlock creative ways of resolving issues.

2) Take control—remember it's not the event which is stressful but your reaction. You can beat the stress response by taking control of the things you can influence with things that are foreseeable.

For example, Mary's boss used to stress her out because he always dumped things on her at the last moment. To reduce her stress levels she decided to proactively manage his diary, and she also called a meeting and told him she would work more effectively if she could have a greater lead time to prepare. He was glad she told him as he had no idea his behavior affected her in this way.

3) Prepare—identify stressful events in advance, and minimize the stressful situation—e.g., get up earlier to avoid running late; go to interviews for jobs you don't want so you can practise, and be less stressed and more skilled when the interview is for a job you really want.

You can also reduce your stress reactions by doing things that build resilience, i.e., if you know you have a heavy load coming up factor in more self-care activities, improving your diet, having a massage, meditating, relaxing or exercising, are just a few strategies.

4) Plan your defence—what is the most realistic solution to your current situation? What options do you have? Plan small, realistic steps: don't try to do everything at once. Choose a few important goals: some things may have to go by the board. Praise yourself when you achieve a goal on the road to success.

"Change the way you look at things and the things you look at will change."
~ **Wayne Dyer, Author**

5) Try a different view—stress experts agree that it is the way that we view events that creates stress. In 2013, research by *The European Heart Journal* found that those who *believed* stress affected their health 'a lot' or 'extremely' had a 50% greater risk of suffering a heart attack, even when researchers adjusted for biological, behavioral and psychological risk factors.

So if you want to reduce your stress levels you need to change the way you view stress and the things that cause you to feel stressed. It's the old glass half full or half empty battle! Here's a few helpful ways to do this:

a) Reframe—change the way you see stressful things and situations, e.g., if a colleague at work is hassling or bullying you, instead of feeling threatened you could be grateful that you have an opportunity to learn and master assertiveness skills and to put these into practice; when you think you have problems, see them as challenges.

b) Do a reality check—look at the here and now: will the things you are worrying about or stressing over ever happen? Where or what is your evidence? If it did happen, what would be the worst-case scenario? Is that so bad? Will it kill you? Is there a way to minimize the risk of a bad outcome?

c) Self-talk—thought is energy, so it's critical to think and talk positive. Compelling research by Dr. Bruce Lipton, a developmental biologist best known for promoting the idea that genes and DNA can be manipulated by a person's beliefs, reveals that thoughts really do become things. If you want to create a positive outcome you must grow and foster positive beliefs—even if in the short-term you have to fake-it-to-make-it. Resist saying things you don't want to make real. Instead of saying, "I can't cope," try replacing it with, "I can do this; I've handled change before," or, "I trust myself to be able to handle this."

To see confirmation of the power of language on your DNA view this clip on YouTube (http://www.youtube.com/watch?v=TWAuc9GivFo), where a water researcher from Japan, Dr. Emoto, demonstrates how thoughts really do change things. His water demonstration shows without doubt how your thoughts and intentions shape the physical world.

Positive messages create shiny, diamond-like reflective qualities while negative thoughts create deformed, collapsed structures with black holes and yellow tinged edges. We know this intuitively every time we're around someone who is negative but many stressed out people don't realize their negative, complaining, or angry energy is toxic to those around them. As Einstein once said, "everything is energy."

d) Don't think in absolutes—you'll only disappoint yourself. Absolute statements like: "I *must* be perfect at everything I do *all the time*," or, "Everyone *must* like me," or "I *always* have to be in control, "is setting yourself up for failure.

These mistaken all-or-nothing beliefs are easily embraced during times of stress, but offer a false sense of security. It's OK, and very normal, not to be perfect.

It's also a myth that we're ever totally in control. Instead of saying, 'I must', try a less absolute statement like, 'I prefer things to be of a high standard', or 'I like to be in control but I accept that this isn't always possible and that's ok too. I'm doing the best I can.'

e) Resist feeling like a victim—let go of negativity, no matter how justified you may feel. Don't focus on any bad aspects. For example, instead of complaining," Why me?" try saying, "It's a pain, but I'll deal with it." Or ask, "How can this problem or set-back turn out for my highest good?"

I really like what Susan Jeffers, the author of, Feel *The Fear and Do It Anyway*, encourages people to say during times of stress, "I constantly remind myself my life is unfolding in a perfect way. I trust the grand design."

6) Increase your coping skills—if you up-skill you'll minimize stress. Lots of people I have coached professionally have benefited from improving their: communication and assertiveness, ability to delegate, self-esteem, confidence and time management skills.

Others have benefited hugely from learning how to meditate. To download a free meditation tip sheet go to my website here: http://www.worklifesolutions.nz/books/career-rescue

Other effective coping strategies may also include exercise or travel, taking breaks during the day, talking worries through, scheduling time off or taking time out. It never fails to amaze me how few people actually take lunch breaks!

What three things could you do to increase your coping skills?

"When you dwell on all the reasons you have to be grateful, you open yourself to receiving even more good—and more good comes to you. As you begin to feel abundant, you'll be willing and able to pass positive things on to others."
~ Oprah Winfrey, Talk Show Host

7) Eliminate negative emotions—as you've already discovered everything, including your emotions, is energy. Negative emotions are toxic, robbing you of optimism and energy, and positive emotions create the opposite results.

One emotion that many clients who are unhappy at work experience is anger. Sometimes that anger is directed at themselves for not making changes earlier.

Anger can often kick in at times of frustration during job hunting activities too, when things don't go successfully.

When you trigger the stress response by getting angry it effectively disengages the cerebral cortex—the thinking part of the brain. That may be fine if you need to launch into defensive combat, but it doesn't help if you need to choose the best response and stop and muse on the merits of your chosen course of action.

Resist making huge life decisions when you're angry.

I knew of a man who made a dramatic change during a time of acute unhappiness. For over 15 years Martin had hated his job. When he sold his shares in his business, an opportunity to reinvent his life appeared.

But lacking awareness of his transferrable skills and alternative career options he opted for self-employment in the same career. He assumed that the added flexibility and autonomy would give him back his mojo. Four years on he's disillusioned and angry.

"I'm a 53-year-old fool. I hate what I do. I hate the person it makes me. I hate my clients: I think they're all pariahs."

In a fit of rage he decided to close down his business, take the hit, and put his house on the market.

'I'll get on a plane and leave. I can't afford to live here,' he said.

At the time, I couldn't help but wonder how different the outcome may have been if he'd been proactive or sought professional help. What if he had spent more time thinking about what else he could do with his considerable skills and talents before he quit his business? What if he'd 'cut his cloth' earlier? I'm sure a more strategic, less dramatic change and reaction decision would have been reached. One with far better consequences.

In saying that, sometimes you have to know when it's time to quit, but planning, preparation and foresight go a long way. I guess you know that or you wouldn't be reading this book.

8) Think and grow positive—tests of brain patterns show that positive thoughts trigger the production of feel-good hormones to areas of the brain responsible for positive emotions.

There is incredibly widespread ignorance of how emotions actually work. People struggle with the idea that we actually choose our emotions.

"He made me angry," one client said defensively. It's impossible for one human being to make another angry, sad, depressed or happy. There is always a point of choice. If you are struggling to deal with negative emotions, seek advice from the experts—remember a problem shared is a problem solved.

Be a guard for your words, thoughts and feelings, and call in the cavalry. Think and grow positive—grab onto anything that makes you feel better about yourself and what you have to offer. I believe in a Higher Power, both within myself and in the unseen world—holding onto my spirituality always comforts me during challenging times.

9) Tap into your passion—Charles Kovess, author of *Passionate People Produce,* describes passion as: 'A source of unlimited energy from the soul that enables people to achieve extraordinary results.'

Often when you're feeling stressed, the things that you love to do are the first things to be traded. When you tap into something you deeply believe in and enjoy you may be amazed at the results.

Passion brings the energy or chi of love, giving you energy, vitality and a heightened sense of well-being. It's one of the greatest stress-busters of all, and promotes the generation of endorphins—feel-good chemicals that will give you an extra spring in your step. Even five minutes a day doing something you love can give you your mojo back.

What may start off as a hobby could very well turn out to be a fulfilling career. Like Brian Clifford, owner of Integrated Pest Management, who had always been fascinated with bugs. After becoming disenchanted with his first career, he opted to follow his passion and became a 'pestie.' He loves the idea of being a white knight coming to people's rescue.

What do you love doing? What inspires you? What makes you feel joyful? Identify these things and make some time to go do it. How could it lead you to a new career?

10) Get moving—during times of stress we can become lethargic. Feeling that we don't even have the energy or time to exercise may lead to feelings of depression as well as increased irritability.

Numerous studies have shown that exercise promotes the production of positive endorphins, which play a key role in making you feel better about yourself and your capacity to cope.

Research out of Princeton University now even suggests that regular physical activity may grow new brain cells. Exercise also helps to activate both hemispheres of your brain—bringing a new perspective as well as greater tolerance to life's stressors.

11) Breathe—under stress our breathing is reversed. Instead of breathing slowly and deeply our breathing tends to become shallower and more rapid. Under extreme stress we can forget to breathe at all. The actress Drew Barrymore had the words 'breathe' tattooed underneath her arm to remind her what to do during times of stress.

In a state of joy and relaxation, you breathe in a deep circular pattern, your heart comes into coherence and you begin to produce alpha brain waves, giving you access to your own natural tranquillizers and antidepressants.

Focusing on your breath and breathing deeply, can bring a state of calm and perspective during times of stress, allowing you to cope more effectively and to slow down or inhibit the stress response.

If you have forgotten how to breathe try this: breathe in deeply for a count of four, and exhale—slowing for a count of eight. Repeat 10 times. Notice how quickly your body and mind relaxes. Try this anywhere, anytime you notice feelings of stress returning and beat the stress response. Or tap into a meditation or yoga class for a mind-body makeover.

12) Tip the balance—it won't come as a surprise that lack of work-life balance increases stress. Research proves that people who organize their whole life around their work are more prone to high levels of stress and the development of post-traumatic embitterment disorder—a malady that covers almost every negative emotion a person can have at work.

Finding and prioritizing time for the things you enjoy is critical if you want to reduce your stress levels. Isolate all the key areas of your life and check to see if you have got the balance right.

13) Keep a food, and mood journal—this is one of the simplest biofeedback, self-help tools available.

> "The only way to keep your health is to eat what you don't want, drink what you don't like, and do what you'd rather not."
> **~ Mark Twain, Author**

Many stress coaches encourage their clients to think of themselves as athletes. If you were a professional athlete, you would know whether you ran better in Nikes or Reeboks, whether your best times came after you ate steak and eggs for breakfast or granola.

Ask yourself, "What am I doing right?" Numerous studies suggest that people who keep journals manage to heal themselves on more than just psychological levels. Keeping track of your food and mood will help reinforce the behaviors that make you feel better, and be stronger about saying no to those which make you feel bad. You'll be more empowered and encouraged to tune into the higher intelligence of your body, mind and spirit.

14) Food for the mind, body and soul—reducing caffeine, alcohol, nicotine and other stimulants is a powerful way to feel better during times of stress. The trouble is that these sorts of stimulants are just the things people feel drawn to.

Like John who hates his job and tries to switch off by hitting the bottle, "I'm going to get a bottle of wine. It's the only way I can cope. I can't do this work without it."

Yet one drink leads to another and another, and before you know it cracks appear.

> "I made a commitment to completely cut out drinking and anything that might hamper me from getting my mind and body together. And the floodgates of goodness have opened upon me, spiritually and financially."
> ~ *Denzel Washington, Actor*

Alcohol is a well documented neurotoxin—a toxic substance that inhibits, damages and destroys the tissues of your nervous system, especially your neurons, the conducting cells of your body's central nervous system.

If you can't knock out alcohol and other stimulants completely at least limit your intake. They all trigger the production of the stress-related hormone adrenaline, which increases the heart rate, prompts your liver to release more sugar into your bloodstream and makes your lungs suck in more oxygen.

While you may get a short-term energy spike or feeling of well-being, in the long run, you'll experience fatigue, low energy levels and even increased anxiety and depression—leading to a vicious cycle of relying on more stimulants to get you through the days and nights.

Dying for a smoke? One of my clients started smoking during a period of stress. "I was bored," she said. "I just wanted to fit in with the people I was working with."

Aside from serious health implications you know about, like lung, brain and throat cancer, smoking robs the blood, muscles, brain and organs of oxygen, causing people to feel light-headed and tired and impeding optimal functioning.

Nicotine also increases levels of adrenaline and creates a vicious cycle of energy highs and lows. Cut down or stop. To help curb cravings, try taking a complex B vitamin supplement.

Mind Food

One of the best things you can also do to improve your stress resilience and well-being, and increase your chances of making a positive and sustainable change, is to improve your food diet. There's a wealth of information on the web, but some of the things I've found really help are:

- Increasing my intake of fresh organic fruit and vegetables

- Reducing meat and dairy and processed foods

- Avoiding too much sugar and artificial energy stimulates

- Cutting out booze

- Seeking professional help to identify allergies

Healthy foods

- It's easy to miss meals when you're busy so opt for healthy snacks such as fruit, brown pitta bread with hummus and vegetable sticks with cubes of cheese, rather than crisps and chocolate

- Eat small but regular meals to sustain energy levels and keep blood sugar levels steady

- Shellfish, particularly oysters, are the richest source of zinc

- Complex carbohydrate foods, wholemeal bread, pasta, wholegrain cereals and brown rice restore depleted energy levels

- Meat and fish contain beneficial amounts of iron, as do green leafy vegetables, dried apricots, lentils and other pulses

- Useful sources of B-group vitamins include whole grains, chicken, fish, eggs, dairy produce, pulses, shellfish and red meat

- Make sure you get sufficient amounts of B-group vitamins, particularly riboflavin, which converts carbohydrates into energy; vitamin B6 essential for energy metabolism; and vitamin B12, required for forming red blood cells that carry oxygen throughout the body

- Help your body absorb more iron by drinking a glass of orange juice once a day with a meal. Vitamin C also helps to boost energy

- Other vital minerals include magnesium, which works with potassium and sodium to ensure the efficient working of muscles, along with zinc, which protects against viral infections that often precede chronic fatigue

- Water plays a vital role in maintaining good health but few of us drink enough. It delivers nutrients around the body, regulates body temperature and transports waste

It's best to choose filtered or natural mineral water to achieve the desired daily amount. Coffee, tea and fizzy drinks contain caffeine, and have a diuretic effect, dehydrating the body.

Herbal teas are healthy, caffeine-free alternatives. Try to drink 6-8 glasses (1.7-2 liters) of water a day to flush out toxins.

Avoid

- Short-term energy boosters, i.e.

- Sugary foods, including biscuits, cakes and chocolate. These also promote short term energy highs, leading to irritability and lethargy

- Alcohol—in large quantities it's draining on your body and mind—although the occasional glass of wine can revive energy levels

- Refined carbohydrates foods like white bread, pasta and rice destabilize energy levels by causing a sharp increase in blood sugar levels

15) **Rest**—when your stress levels are high and you get depressed, angry, tense, lethargic or begin to experience tension headaches etc., that should be a very simple biofeedback signal that you are better off stopping, re-evaluating your choices and taking some time out.

Sometimes this can be easier said than done. In our overachiever, overstimulated society, where many people spend more hours every week with their eyes riveted to their iPhone, instead of spending quality time on their own or with family and friends, the whole concept of stopping and resting to restore ourselves is almost unusual. But resting to replenish is essential to well-being.

We're pushing ourselves all day long with energy that we don't have. The most common complaint people go to the doctor for is fatigue. Research conducted by a company helping people suffering from adrenal fatigue claims that 80% of people don't have as much energy as they'd like to have. "It's because we're pushing and using caffeine, sugar and energy drinks and nicotine and stress for energy rather than running on our own energy."

Rest allows the adrenal glands to restore, enabling cortisol levels to return to normal. Long-term stress and long-term cortisol overload can lead to adrenal fatigue and burn-out, altering your hormonal profile, and making it more difficult to return to the real, inspired, happy and creative you.

Give yourself permission to take time every day and every week to have fun, rest your mind and rest your body. This is a spiritual principle taught very well in the Bible, but even the most spiritual people often feel they are worthless unless they are doing something every waking hour of the day, or connected with everyone on email and all the social media platforms.

Yet, if you look back at some of the symptoms of stress you will see that people's cognitive or thinking capabilities actually reduce. Stressed people make more mistakes, forget more and take longer to achieve less. So taking a break is a great way to revitalize your performance and to work smarter not harder.

Do less, achieve more

When I was feeling stressed many years ago following a period of intense personal and professional change, I knew I needed time out. At first I didn't think I could afford it. Instead of staying stuck I started to think proactively. "How could I afford it?" I asked my higher self.

I rented out my house to short-term holiday people on holidayhomes.com. While people were staying in my house I stayed at a friend's holiday house—rent free.

I rescheduled all my appointments and cleared my diary for three weeks.

While away I scheduled no more than two hours a day for work-related activities. I couldn't afford to go completely cold turkey, but at least I avoided working my normal 12-hour days. I made sure I minimized interruptions by turning off my phone and shutting down the laptop.

How could you schedule some time out? Add this to your stress-busting plan discussed at the end of the chapter.

"Happiness is a butterfly, which when pursued, is always beyond your grasp, but which, if you will sit down quietly may alight upon you."
~ *Nathaniel Hawthorne, Author*

16) Laugh—inject some more laughter into your life. Laughter and humor are great tonics during stressful times. Go and see a funny movie, rent a stack of whacky DVDs, go to a comedy show or watch one on YouTube, and hang out with people who know how to have a good time, or go to a Laughing Yoga class. Taking life too seriously is a recipe for illness.

17) Finally, normalize stress—know that change of any kind, exciting or worrying, adds to stress levels. Take heed of most of the previous stress-busting strategies and create your own stress-busting plan in the following space.

18) Meditation—The regular practice of meditation is scientifically proven to reduce stress and anxiety and to increase well-being. Meditating also promotes intuitive insight, unconditional love and personal spiritual experiences. Some popular meditation techniques include transcendental meditation, breathing meditations, and walking meditations. Meditating can be as simple as sitting quietly for 20 minutes focusing on one thing—whether this is a number you repeat over and over, e.g., "one, one, one," or focusing on your breath as many of the Buddhist meditations do.

19) Massage—So many people mistakenly think massage is an indulgence rather than a health-behavior. Some of the many benefits include: reduced stress and higher levels of neuroendocrine and immune functioning—which means better hormonal balance and more immunity to disease and illness. Some studies also suggest that a one hour massage results in benefits equivalent to a 6 hour sleep. Sounds good to me, especially when I'm feeling fatigued.

20) **Essential oils.** Another effective tool in your stress-busting kit is aromatherapy. Drop a few drops of one of the blends below onto a tissue and inhale for instant calm.

- Blend #1: Three drops Clary Sage, one drop Lemon, one drop Lavender

- Blend #2: Two drops Roman Chamomile, two drops Lavender, one drop Vetiver

- Blend #3: Three drops Bergamot, one drop Geranium, one drop Frankincense

- Blend #4: Three drops Grapefruit, one drop Jasmine, one drop Ylang Ylang

Action Question: Are You Bored?

Did you know that being bored, under-challenged or not being able to do the things you care about are huge sources of stress? What's boring you about you current situation? How can you create some more challenge, learning or excitement, into your workday?

"Are you bored with life? Then throw yourself into some work you believe in with all your heart, live for it. Die for it, and you will find happiness that you had thought could never be yours."
~ *Dale Carnegie, Motivational Guru*

The Self-Care Quiz

Take the following self-care quiz to assess how well you're already looking after yourself. Your responses will also highlight what you need to add into your stress management plan.

The aim of this check-up is to develop awareness of current lifestyle factors which may be positively or negatively impacting your health and wellbeing. Read each item and then give it a rating depending on how often the item applies to you NOW. There are no right or wrong answers—just an honest assessment.

1 = almost always

2 = often

3 = sometimes

4 = occasionally

5 = almost never

1. I get at least two balanced meals a day

2. I get 7-8 hours' sleep at least four nights per week

3. I receive affection regularly

4. I have at least one relative/friend within 50kms on whom I can rely

5. I exercise to the point of perspiration at least twice a week

6. I smoke less than five cigarettes a day (non-smokers score 1)

7. I take fewer than five alcoholic drinks a week (non-drinkers score 1)

8. My weight is OK from a health point of view

9. My income is adequate to meet basic expenses

10. I get strength from my beliefs and feel comfortable with my views of the universe and my place in it

11. I attend social activities regularly

12. I have a network of friends and acquaintances

13. I have friends to confide in personally, deeply

14. I'm in good health

15. I'm able to be open about my feelings

16. I have intimate conversations with people I live with

17. I do something for fun at least once a week

18. I'm able to organize my time effectively

19. I drink fewer than three cups of coffee, tea or coke a day

20. I take quiet times for myself during the day

Scoring:

Calculate your total. A general picture of your self-care status will emerge from this scale:

Less than 40 Indicates great self-care, good modelling for others

41 to 60 Fairly good self-care

61 to 70 Talking health but modelling sickness

71 plus Take time to look after yourself before it is too late

Any items with a score of 3, 4 or 5 suggest that you may need to re-evaluate this area of your life. You will probably need to make some changes. Some may feel out of your reach, even impossible, but you never know what can happen once you make it a priority.

> "The best six doctors anywhere—and no one can deny it—are sunshine, water, rest, and air, exercise and diet. These six will gladly you attend if only you are willing Your mind they'll ease, your will they'll mend, and charge you not a shilling."
> ~ *Nursery rhyme quoted by Wayne Fields, Professor and Writer*

Action Task! Your Stress-busting Plan

Go back over the previous pages and identify some things you can start, stop, do more and do less of to get rid of excess stress from your life. Jot these down in your journal:

1) I will start...

2) I will stop...

3) I will do less...

4) I will do more...

Remember angry Martin? Eventually he sought career counselling and developed a stress management plan to help him build a strong foundation for success. A few of the changes he made included:

He started: running; eating organic foods; meditating; reading self-empowerment books; working on a plan for career fulfilment; pushing back on unreasonable client demands; taking quiet time out for himself and spending time alone in nature.

He stopped: working weekends; drinking alcohol; watching TV, reading negative media; responding to emails and texts and calls immediately; working with clients he didn't enjoy; complaining; angry, explosive rants and raves; infecting everyone else with his bad moods; blaming others.

He did less: work after hours; Facebook surfing; drinking coffee; emails—picking up the phone instead; saying no to social get-togethers; spending money he hadn't yet earned.

He did more: focusing on what was going well and listing gratitudes; taking control of the things he could influence; spending time in the garden; planning holidays and quality time with his son; taking time out to focus on his hobbies and passions; controlling his emotions; taking responsibility; creating systems and templates that allowed him to work smarter not harder; and delegating.

I hope this chapter has given you some tools to deal effectively with any stress you may be suffering and also reminds you of the need to make positive changes in your life.

You may need to refer to this chapter again as you prepare to make changes in the future.

"Organs evolve in response to necessity. Therefore increase your necessity."
~ Jalad-ad-din-ai Rumi,13th Century Mystic

What You've Learned So Far

- A degree of stress is a normal part of living. It gives you the energy you need to enjoy life and feel excitement and enthusiasm.

- Too much stress, however, can drown all the good feelings and create illness, depression, tension and self-doubt. Left unresolved too much stress can erode your will to live.

- Many people don't realize they're stressed and nearing burnout until it is too late. They soldier on or grit their teeth and bear whatever is causing the pain. They ignore early, medium and red alert warning signs that their body is giving them.

- Tune into your body barometer and listen for the physical, emotional, cognitive and behavioral signs of too much stress.

- Eliminate excess stress and build resilience by: identifying what's stressing you out; taking control; anticipating and preparing in advance; planning realistic solutions; trying a different view; reframing; doing a reality check; talking positively; resisting the urge to feel like a victim; increasing your coping skills; eliminating negative emotions; tapping into your passion; moving; breathing; regaining some balance; keeping a food, and mood journal; resting; and laughing.

- Remind yourself that stress is a normal part of life—it's how you handle it that counts. Create a stress management plan and proactively manage your stress levels.

- Love it, don't leave it. Sometimes removing sources of stress in either your work or private life can mean falling back in love with your job.

What's Next?

Now that we've looked at the factors driving and supporting your desire for change, and highlighted strategies to boost your spirit, let's get dreaming! The next chapter, "It All Begins with an Idea" will ignite your imagination and help you rediscover a sense of possibility for the future.

IT ALL BEGINS WITH AN IDEA

"I propose a radical, yet ancient notion: To build the life you want—complete with inner satisfaction, personal meaning and rewards—create the work you love."
~ *Marsha Sinetar, Author*

Many of my clients have said they could do anything if they only knew what it was. Finding the job of your dreams and standing out from the crowd begins with an idea, a dream or a hunch about what you would love to do and why.

However, this is not the way that many of us have been conditioned to think about careers.

Traditional methods used to choose careers like checklists and assessments are being transformed by some creative thinking. Listen to my interview on Radio New Zealand—we're discussing this very thing: http://worklifesolutions.nz/media/tv-radio-and-youtube/

Did you know that at the age of four, 96% of children think they can be anything they want to be, but by the age of 18 only 4% of them still believe it?

As people grow up, they tend to close down the sense of possibility and trade in their dreams for a steady pay check and a proper job.

However, times are changing. An increasing awareness of the power of creativity is changing the way people choose jobs and careers.

For too long, the role of emotions has been left out of making decisions. After years of conditioning that work is something to be endured, not loved, it makes sense. But now these outmoded ways of thinking are being shed.

Thankfully now more than any time in the past, people have far more choice about the type of work they can do and where and how they do it.

As Nick Williams, author of *The Work You Were Born To Do*, shares in the foreword of this book, "too few of us have been bought up to believe that it is possible to make our living doing something we love, that lights our hearts up and stirs our passions. This is what I call the work we were born to do, and is our true work. To find your true work is a great blessing, one of life's greatest blessings I believe. And to be paid for your work rather than work for pay is one of life's greatest joys."

Are you ready to find your greatest joy?

The exercises in this chapter will help you free up your creativity and think more broadly about career options. They will also help you to bring into greater awareness your own criteria for job satisfaction. Remember to approach these exercises as an explorer.

The purpose is to help you think outside the square and to think laterally about possible career options. You do not have to make firm choices, or commit to any action that you may not feel ready for.

You may not even feel you have enough information about yourself to complete the exercises. Don't worry. The main thing is to start the process of creating your dream role by planting the seeds of insight and inspiration.

Get Creative—Dream And Explore

Discovering your great joy and the work you were born to do requires allowing yourself to dream and explore. It requires tuning down the rational mind for a while and engaging the right side of your brain, and listening to your intuition and the stirrings of your heart.

Discovering your great joy and the work you were born to do requires a commitment and willingness to tap into your subconscious where unexpressed desires dwell. It requires allowing yourself to dream and imagine a reality that doesn't yet exist. It requires being creative.

To do this with work, you have to be prepared to challenge current assumptions and allow yourself to dream about what could be possible.

"Imagination is more important than any other trait for my work and such an easy skill to develop. Never look where you think you should, creation of a new idea is simply combining two or more existing concepts together. A new idea can be either unfamiliar, silly or both."
~ Mark Olsen, Artist

The Heart Of Creativity

Many people get caught up in the classical definitions of an artist when they think about creativity, but you don't have to be an artist, painter or sculptor to be creative. Imagining what doesn't yet exist and then bringing it into being lies at the heart of creativity.

The American Heritage Dictionary of the English Language defines the ability to create as: to make or cause to be or to become; bring into existence; pursue a creative activity; be engaged in a creative activity; invest with a new title, office, or rank; create by artistic means; create or manufacture a man-made product.

Creativity is about...

- Imagining what could be
- Dreams, hopes and desires
- Challenging the status quo
- Being willing to change
- Thinking outside the square
- Drawing outside the lines
- Bringing something into existence
- Innovation and new ideas
- Taking risks, trials and errors
- A wish for something better
- Tailoring for changing needs
- Uniqueness

- Producing something

- Designing new products and services.

Lighten Up!

Let go of needing to know all the answers, finding a cure for cancer, ending hunger, solving problems or creating the job you know for sure you will love.

Creativity, dreaming and exploring is simply a brain-dumping process that helps stimulate new ideas and connections. Start with an open, playful attitude—you can always get serious later.

Action Tasks! Generating Ideas

Here are a few tips to help you unleash a sense of possibility and tap into your creative self. Jot some initial thoughts in response to the below and add further insights in your passion journal.

1) Clone yourself

Imagine you've just been cloned. You are now five people! Each of you has gone in a completely different career direction. There are no constraints—money is not an issue. You can get any job you want and you're getting all the experience you need.

What would each person be doing or willing to try? Isolate and list the key elements that make each of the five careers listed below satisfying to each clone.

Carol a disillusioned counsellor whose role was made redundant, wanted to get away from always hearing about people's problems. She came to me for coaching as she was finding it hard to identify roles which would excite her.

Before coaching, she wrote, "I'm starting to question whether I'm doing the right thing applying for jobs at the moment. It's stressful and I'm afraid I may end up in a role that I don't want. I'm feeling quite conflicted at the moment."

I thought the cloning exercise would be a great way to stimulate her sense of possibility and remind her of the things that gave her joy. Joy, one of my other clients reminded me recently, is the fruit of your spirit.

At first Carol was skeptical. It all sounded very impractical. I encouraged her to let go of her rational mind and play with possibilities. Once we had a few ideas down, I reassured her, we could look at 'concrete' career options then.

Her clones included, being; A financially successful global coach; a non-fiction writer; an artist travelling the world; a creative educator; and the creator of a thriving community.

We then isolated all the elements that made these roles fulfilling to each clone and stretched the boundaries further by exploring how these clones could combine into what I call a 'career combo'—a combination of careers strengthened by a core theme and united under one umbrella.

"I'm feeling excited," she said, as together we set about planning how she could make her career combo a reality.

Clone yourself by downloading the free worksheet from my website, here: http://worklifesolutions.nz/books/career-rescue/

If you identified a role that combines many jobs or have just invented a new job title, begin to think about where you could find a market or outlet for it. It may be that you do what I call a 'career combo'—a little bit of this and a little bit of that!

2) Take what already exists and copy it.

Much of what we have learned we copied from people close to us, like our parents, or teachers, before we put our own unique own stamp on it.

Who could you copy? Identify someone who is working in a field you feel you would enjoy and learn as much as possible about what they did to achieve success.

When I was stuck in a career trap I was inspired by the career counsellor who was helping me and I began to wonder, 'how could I do that?'

I looked at her skills and background and asked her what it would take to be like her, and what training she would or wouldn't recommend.

I then set out to forge my path in a similar way—even learning the interactive drawing therapy techniques I'd found so liberating when she first got me to draw that bird trapped in the cage yearning to fly.

3) Take what already exists and modify it.

'Job sculpting' is a technique from the Harvard Business School that involves tapping into the psychology of work satisfaction and matching people to jobs that allow their interests to be expressed.

How could you tailor your current role to increase the amount of time spent on activities that make you happy? If you are unemployed, how could you use the skills and experiences from your previous role to create your best-fit career?

4) Totally reinvent the wheel.

How could you tap into economic, demographic and social changes to create a product or service that really excites you and for which there may be a future demand?

When Elizabeth Barbalich founded her successful company *Antipodes* she tuned into the growing interest in New Zealand products and natural skin care, free of animal testing.

> "Designing is not the abstract power exercised by a genius. It is simply the arranging of how work shall be done."
> ~ **W. R. Lethaby, Architect**

Action Tasks! Use Emotion Not Reason Alone

Human beings are fuelled by emotion, not by reason. Studies have shown that when the emotional centers of our brains are damaged in some way we don't lose the ability to laugh or cry, we lose the ability to make decisions.

Harness the inspiring and motivational power of feelings by trying some of the following techniques:

1) Visualize your way to success. Some people have estimated that we have 80,000 thoughts a day and up to 80% of these are negative. Keep your mind on what you do want and off what you don't!

See your way to success. Create a mental image of what you want to accomplish or obtain by imagining the desired outcome in your mind. At the same time, repeat a positive, present-tense affirmation about the goal.

"If you want to be creative, stay in part a child, with the creativity and invention that characterizes children before they are deformed by adult society."
~ *Jean Piaget Educational Psychologist*

Don't get stuck on the term 'visualization.' Different people have different dominant senses. The most common is the sense of sight. This is why for most people the process of visualization works well.

Others, however, may have a dominant sense of touch or hearing or smell. These people may have difficulty 'visualizing' but may be able to accurately imagine sounds, smells or feelings.
Work with whatever works for you but try to engage all the senses by imagining what you will see, what you will hear, what scents surround you, how surfaces feel etc.

2) Create a dream board, passion journal or even a whole wall filled with images that inspire you and remind you of the things you want to manifest.

According to mind-mapping and creativity expert Tony Buzan, we think in images not words. Surround yourself with images that symbolize or reflect the things you want to create. Allow these images to inspire and excite you. Add a dose of color and engage all your senses.

I was clearing out some of my old journals one year when I came across something I had written back in 2000. "I will live in a house that is elevated with lots of sun and which is surrounded by trees. It will be elegant and streamlined, with simplicity at its core and feng-shuied to make sure it is the best it can be."

What amazed me was not what I had written but the astonishing realization that seven years later I was actually living in the house I had created in my imagination. I have done the same thing in my career.

'I dream I'm on vacation, it's the perfect career for me.' These lyrics from a song by the Eagles was a theme around which manifesting my perfect career centered. Clarifying my skills, values and interests provided further focus as did confirming my life purpose and the longer-term goals I have for myself, my partner and my family.

We now live in a lifestyle property in The Bay Of Islands, in New Zealand—a popular holiday destination, working from home with clients all over the world. Sometimes when I'm coaching a client over the phone I walk around the garden. It's so much fun—work always feels like a vacation.

Gathering images of the ingredients of career satisfaction, including where I wanted to live and work, helped me see my way to career success and directed my job creation activities much more efficiently. Now that's powerful creativity!

It's also one of the principals of the Law of Attraction made infamous by the DVD *The Secret*. But guess what? There is no secret! What there is instead is a lack of conscious awareness about how to tap into the Law of Attraction to make your dreams and goals real.

You can make your goals holistic too, as I once did in my dream wall. The images reminded me about the importance of family, spirituality, relationships and longer-term life goals. They remind me of the importance of only doing work that allows me to balance my needs and to do work that is life-affirming.

The importance of thinking holistically will help you affirm your best-fit career—you'll know what other things are important to you when choosing or creating a career.

To learn more about this powerful technique watch me demonstrating it on television here:

http://worklifesolutions.nz/media/tv-radio-and-youtube/

3) Maintain the faith! Stay positive and keep away from cynics. Tap into the awesome power of meditation, yoga and a spiritual faith based perspective to help you maintain a positive expectancy, manage stress and increase your intuitive, creative powers.

Julia Cameron, an active artist and author of *The Artist's Way* and another thirty or so fiction and non-fiction books, advocates relinquishing too much effort and turning energy instead from one of stressful striving, to cultivating faith and trust.

Prayer, gratitude, acceptance and unwavering belief that everything happens for a reason, are just some of the many strategies she encourages people to embrace.

If faith is something you'd like to cultivate, you'll find them throughout the Career Rescue series. You may like to check out Julia's book *Faith and Will,* or find your own sources.

4) **Associate only with positive, success-oriented people**. Get around winners. Fly with the eagles. You can't fly with the eagles if you keep scratching with the turkeys. Get away from the go-nowhere types and above all stay away from negative people.

If you've got a negative boss, or are surrounded by toxic co-workers seriously consider changing jobs. Associating on a regular basis with negative people zaps your energy and can condemn you to a life of dissatisfaction and underachievement.

Who inspires you? Add pictures of inspirational people to your image board or journal.

5) Be prepared to do the hard yards. Pursuing your dreams isn't always easy—if it was, more people would be doing it. What are you prepared to give up in order to achieve your desires? Free time? Money? Short-term pain? TV? Facebook? Laziness? Comfort? Guarantees?

How will you feel when you have achieved your dreams? Remind yourself of these feelings regularly.

6) Trust your gut! As Einstein once said, "The intuitive mind is a sacred gift and the rational mind is a faithful servant. We have created a society that honors the servant and has forgotten the gift."

Allow your intuition to guide you to the higher ground as Oprah does: "My business skills have come from being guided by my higher self or my intuition. I am who I am today because of... intuition, my ability to feel what is right for me and allowing that to be the strongest guide in my life. Intuition is akin to God. It is akin to being led by that which is greater than yourself. My intuition, my intention and my passion have allowed me to be who I am and will take me to higher ground..."

Everyone is intuitive—many of us have just forgotten how to listen. As a life and career coach and holistic, energy psychologist I've always believed deep down my clients have always known what they wanted to do with their life.

Often what was missing was the courage to listen and then take confident steps toward their dreams. Intuitively I always 'knew' I could create a career that felt like a vacation. Initially, rationally I had no idea how, but I made it my mission to find the answers.

Listen to life's whispers and act on your intuition. What is your intuition telling you to do, be or have?

"A hunch is creativity trying to tell you something."
~ *Frank Capra, Film-maker*

Action Questions: Dare to Dream

As author George Bernard Shaw once said, "Imagination is the beginning of creation. You imagine what you desire, you will what you imagine, and at last you create what you will."

Try answering the following questions to unlock some of your dreams, and bring into being all the things you yearn for:

- What have you always wanted to do but never thought you could?

- What would you do if you knew you couldn't fail?

- When you were a child what did you dream you would be when you grew up?

"It's not your work to make anything happen. It's your work to dream it and let it happen. Law of Attraction will make it happen. In your joy, you create something, and then you maintain your vibrational harmony with it, and the Universe must find a way to bring it about. That's the promise of the Law of Attraction."
~ *Abraham Hicks, Author*

8) Build it. Take a leaf from professional architects and build a model of your ideal job. Play with some ideas starting from the ground up. Create your ideal office space in every aspect, including the furnishings, people, setting (home or big city etc.). If you can't build your ideal job physically, sketch it or create a 'story board.'

9) Act as if. Take a job idea you are considering, or have always wondered what it would be like, and act as if you are doing that role. Dress the part and tell people about what you want to do as though you are already doing it.

One of my clients was struggling to get into a new industry due to lack of experience. I encouraged him to get out of his track pants and dress as though he was already a media and communications expert. I also suggested he have a card designed that announced his desired job title perfectly. He also changed his voicemail. Now instead of, "Hi, Rob here—leave a message," callers were greeted with, "Hello, you've reached Rob Murray, Communications and Media Consultant..."

Soon enough fantasy caught up with reality and he is now doing the job he dreamed of. Another option is to shadow someone who is in the role you are considering to get a feel for what it's like.

> "Be the change you want to see."
> ~ *Mahatma Gandhi, Leader*

10) **Be provocative!** Provocation is a favored technique of creative guru and best-selling author Edward De Bono. It involves putting forward ideas you think are absurd in order to move your thinking forward.

Sometimes when you allow yourself to think of the most ridiculous, wild ideas you free yourself from constraints.

What if...

I remember running a career workshop in a large government organization and getting workshop participants to do the cloning exercise described earlier. One guy clearly thought this was a ridiculous idea, and just to prove that there was no way the exercise would be useful he wrote down that one of his clones would be an SIS agent.

"There's no way that will happen," he scoffed. Well, he nearly fell over when someone next to him said he had seen them advertising for agents in the paper that morning!

When you think about your next job what are some of the most absurd or ridiculous things you can think of? Record your ideas in your passion journal. Are they really so absurd? Do any excite you? How could you make any of them a reality?

The Picture of Success: From Computer Sales to Renown Artist

A former computer salesman, Mark Olsen's creative bent emerged while dining at a restaurant one year. "I saw some paintings on the wall and said to my wife, I could do better than that."

So he set out to achieve just that. The first attempts were shocking, he confesses. But undeterred and fuelled with a newly found passion to create he set about learning as much as he could about the art of creativity.

Primarily self-taught Mark made a determined effort to perfect his art. He spent time reading up on the process and studying the styles of other artists he admired. De-stressing by spending time in his personal flotation chamber (a light- and sound-proof tank filled with water) provided further inspiration.

Copycatting his way to success by studying the styles of his three favorite artists (Picasso, Modigliani and William Dobell) Mark blended the three to come up with his own unique style.

He enjoyed the process so much that he decided he wanted to make it a full-time career. "There was no question I was going to be this poor, stricken artist. I have no desire to live on the bones of my arse," he said.

Mark created a strong picture of his preferred future by imagining himself 20 years from that moment as a 60-year-old experiencing huge success.

It was clear he wanted to be a household name with strong sales around the world. Realizing that without a plan his dream of artistic success would not happen, he studied best-selling artists and, applying a strong marketing approach, set out to create his own brand.

Mark didn't wait for the art world to come to him. He went to the art world. He set himself big challenging goals including an exhibition at a prestigious London gallery—aiming low and settling for less was never on his radar. As they say, if you don't ask you don't get and as luck would have it a sudden cancellation of an exhibition created a well-timed and very fortuitous opportunity for Mark to have a solo show. Sales were so good that Mark quit his job in IT and has been earning a living as a full-time artist ever since.

Ron Espkamp of Exhibitions Gallery says, "Mark is an inspiration both as an artist and as a person. He has in a very short period established himself not only as one of New Zealand's greatest portrait artists but as an artist to watch on the international stage. Mark's success and distinctive style of painting have been a culmination of his passion, self-belief, determination, thirst for knowledge and extremely strong work ethic."

The things Mark has learnt as an artist are applicable to many people wanting to create a new picture of success for their work and their lives. A few of these creative tips are below. You can see more on Mark's website:

http://www.markolsen-artist.com/whativelearnt.html

- To think as big as I can, never wait for the right time
- Surround myself with people that support me, avoid those who don't
- Take action everyday
- Start by being wrong and new ideas appear.

"Your power to choose the direction of your life allows you to reinvent yourself, to change your future, and to powerfully influence the rest of creation."
~ *Dr. Stephen R Covey, Author*

Creative Jobs

One of my friends is a barrister, but he prefers to call himself "a thinker"—in this way recognizing the blend of creative and logical skills he brings to his role. Another man I know calls himself 'an encorporator'—he's an architect, teacher, designer—amongst many of the creative hats he wears in his roles.

Here are some other jobs where people's true creative instincts are encouraged to flourish within a commercial environment:

- Futurist
- Brand Manager
- Strategy Manager
- Director of Business Development
- Business Architect
- PR/Communications Manager
- Graphic Designer
- Interior Designer
- Social Media Planner
- Blogger
- Change Consultant
- Product Designer
- App Developer

Naturally this is not an exhaustive list. Can you think of any others that you'd like to explore?

Action Task! Keep a Look Out

If a creative role appeals to you keep an eye on future trends and look out for jobs and organizations where creativity and innovation are core role requirements. Or do as I once did, either find an organization you'd like to work for and create a role for them; or employ yourself and start your own business.

Ideas Are Big Business

Your ability and willingness to think outside the square is a highly marketable skill. It's not just the standard creative industries such as the movies and the arts that are tapping into creativity.

As international competition continues to increase, organizations are always looking for people who can help them innovate, read trends and stay ahead of their competitors.

What You've Learned So Far

- It all begins with an idea when it comes to creating more happiness in work and in life.

- Many people confess that they don't know what they want and where to begin when it comes to getting more happiness at work.

- Leveraging off the power of creativity is a great place to start, and essential in this modern age. Many of the jobs that exist now will be redundant in the future, and future jobs are yet to be created.

- An increasing awareness of the power of creativity is transforming the way people choose jobs and careers.

- Regaining the sense of possibility and adventure that we had as children is an essential part of awakening desire, creating a picture of success for the future and making concrete plans of achievement.

- Discovering what you want means devoting time to dream and explore first. It means listening to your heart and honouring your intuition. It means being creative.

- Everyone has the potential to be creative. Creativity is simply the ability to bring something into existence. It's a skill, like any other, that can be acquired and perfected.

- Open-mindedness, and a willingness to question the unquestionable, is an essential part of generating new possibilities.

- True creativity stems from, and flames, the embers of desire—it's emotionally charged. Everything begins with an idea. Let go of rational, linear thinking and dare to dream. Let your imagination soar.

> "All successful men and women are big dreamers. They imagine what their future could be, ideal in every respect, and then they work everyday toward their distant vision, that goal or purpose."
> ~ *Brian Tracy, Motivational Guru*

What's Next?

You've heard the call, you're feeling motivated to make a change for the better and some excitement to get moving.

You've awakened your dreams, strengthened your ability to think laterally and creatively, and have some good ideas about what you would like to be doing career-wise. But that's only the beginning...

EPILOGUE

It's time to take a leap of faith and go for your dream.

I hope you have found a few useful tips in this book to fuel the embers of your desires and to help you stay on track. The world needs you and eagerly awaits the fulfilment of your dreams!

I always believe that I should practice what I preach and so you can be sure that many of the strategies and techniques I have shared with you are ones I have put into practice myself. Writing this book is a case in point. It really was a labor of love that had its seeds in the culmination and intersection of my talents, my interests, my motivations and external drivers. Life kept telling me that this was a book I not only wanted to write but was called to write.

I did get off track—several times. External factors like juggling work, bills that needed paying and family commitments, and the odd crisis that absorbed much of my energy temporarily diverted me away from this, my path with heart.

I've also spent time and money investing in new skills—proving that often your calling is something you grow into.

I've learnt about the spiritually motivating power of living to a purpose and strengthened my intuitive powers in the process.

I've been inspired by the American singer, Meatloaf. His mission to find a producer for his album *Bat Out of Hell*, is such an inspirational story about perseverance, failure and ultimate success.

Plus, I've followed one of my muses Richard Branson, whose wise words, "If it's not fun I'm not doing it" have reminded me to always work with joy.

In the days leading up to the completion of this book, so many synchronicities have occurred that have left me in no doubt that the universe is bringing together the resources necessary for me to have my dream. The latest thing to have occurred is an employment alert I received by email. It signaled the potential end of retirement as we once knew it, and highlighted the fact that many people whether by choice or through necessity will continue to work into their 70's, 80's, 90's and beyond—reminding me how this book is needed by so many people.

What is my dream? Well, I have several but one of the most important is that by writing this book I have helped you gain the clarity, confidence, courage and inspiration to live your dreams.

I dream that people like you and those you love can be truly happy when they go to work, and that your happiness will spread the seeds of joy amongst all you meet.

I dream that one day the current research that states that less than 10% of people are living their passions will be surpassed by new data showing that over 80% of people are happy at work and in life.

Is this really dreaming? Decide for yourself. Perhaps, this book will help you to turn your dreams of a happy working life into a fulfilling reality.

Thank you for allowing me to go on this journey with you.

Wishing you everything your heart desires.

Passionately and happily yours,
Cassandra

P.S. What makes you happy?

In response to feedback from readers, I wrote a new book in the *Mid-Life Career Rescue* series called, *What Makes You Happy*. It became an instant #1 best-seller on Amazon.

In *What Makes You Happy* I'll help you clarify what you need from work to be fulfilled. Plus, we'll dive deeper into discovering your vein of gold—the strengths, gifts and natural talents you have to give the world.

Practical tips, inspiration and lessons learned from other successful mid-life career changers will help you manifest, create and take practical and inspired steps so you can live your best life. With vision, planning and perseverance, working with purpose, passion and profit can be yours.

Download sample chapters, or purchase *Mid-Life Career Rescue:What Makes You Happy* from Amazon here: getBook.at/MakeYouHappy

Available in paperback and print.

Is It Time To Quit?

Look For The Tell-Tale Signs

Most people who want to quit their jobs behave in ways that are noticeably different than employees who are happy at work.

Try the following Ready to Quit Quiz to see how many of these 'quitting signs' are true for you.

The Ready To Quit Quiz

1. You find it hard to get out of bed in the morning.

2. You're often late for work.

3. Once you arrive at work, it takes you a while to actually get started working.

4. You sit at your desk and daydream.

5. You have less patience with customers or co-workers than you used to.

6. You spend time at work doing personal tasks.

7. You look at job websites on the Internet when you're at work.

8. You get impatient with rules and red tape on the job.

9. You take longer breaks than you should.

10. When you have to phone people as part of your job you spend more time chatting than you need to.

11. You feel tired during the workday.

12. You don't bother mentioning concerns to the boss or HR because it's usually a waste of time.

13. If you leave the office during the day, you take your time getting back to work.

14. You do the minimum amount of work required.

15. You check the time throughout the day to see how close to quitting time it is.

16. You feel bored at work.

17. You 'kill time' during the day by chatting with co-workers or doing other non-essential tasks.

18. You schedule medical and other personal appointments during working hours.

19. You start getting ready to leave work before knock off time.

20. You're out the door as soon as it's quitting time.

21. You spend a lot of time complaining about what's not going right at work.

22. On the weekends you look at the job classifieds or surf job websites

23. You've called in sick when you could've worked.

24. You complain about your job.

25. You have trouble sleeping on Sunday nights because you're thinking about having to go back to work.

26. When you're on holidays you dread going back to work.

Scoring:

If you answered "yes" to more than six but less than 14 of these statements, you are moderately dis-satisfied. While you're not ready to quit, you could benefit from getting clearer about what makes you happy at work. Then you may be able to take steps to change things for the better. If not, it may be time to quit.

If you answered "yes" to 14 but less than 20 of these statements you have a great level of dis-satisfaction with your current job. If you can't improve things for the better, it may be time to make a move.

If you answered "yes" 20 of these statements—why are you still working there? It's time to identify career options that you will enjoy and be successful at.

FURTHER RESOURCES

E-BOOKS

More of Cassandra's practical and inspiring workbooks on a range of career and life enhancing topics can be found on her Amazon Author Page.

Navigate to: https://www.amazon.com/Cassandra-Gaisford/e/B016LGWES2

NEWSLETTERS

For inspiring tools and helpful tips subscribe to Cassandra's free newsletters here:

http://www.worklifesolutions.nz/home

Sign up now and receive a free eBook!

LIFE AND CAREER COACHING

A Worklife Solutions coach is available whenever, and for as long as you need. We provide Skype, phone or email coaching. You can schedule a regular appointment or simply call at times of stress, confusion or when you just need a motivational kick-start.

Navigate to: http://www.worklifesolutions.nz/services-for-individuals

TRAIN TO BE A COACH

Cassandra is passionate about helping people find work they love and still pay the bills! If you share her passion and are seeking work that is fulfilling, financially rewarding and flexible becoming a career and life coach may be just what you have been looking for!

Work with passion!

Contact us to become an accredited:

- Career coach

- Life coach

- Happy at Work coach

- Creativity coach.

Navigate to: http://www.worklifesolutions.nz/coach-training

SURF THE NET

www.aarp.org/work—information and tools to help you stay current, connected and connected with what's hot and what's not in today's workplace.

www.lifereimagined.org—loads of inspiration and practical tips to help you maximize your interests and expertise, personalized and interactive.

www.whatthebleep.com—a powerful and inspiring site emphasizing quantum physics and the transformational power of thought.

www.heartmath.org - comprehensive information and tools to help you access your intuitive insight and heart based knowledge. Validated and supported by science-based research.

www.eeotrust.co.nz—contains a variety of articles about issues related to mature workers.

www.thirdage.com—contains a variety of holistic articles and online classes designed to help mid-lifers get the most from their lives.

www.personalitytype.com—owned by the authors of Do What You Are: Discover the Perfect Career for You through the Secrets of Personality Type—this site focuses on expanding your awareness of your own type and that of others—including children and partners. This site also contains many useful links.

www.careers.govt.nz—a comprehensive site funded by The NZ government to help you make career decisions. research jobs and salaries, find out about training, and access free resources.

www.careerjet.co.nz—an employment search engine allowing you to access thousands of jobs globally.

www.seek.co.nz—sign up for job alerts or search their current vacancies.

www.jobs.govt.nz—you'll find a wide range of Government jobs on this site.

www.monster.com—go global on this website. Search for international or local positions and access a wide range of career related resources.

Staying in touch

I invite you to share your stories and experiences in our Career Rescue Community. We'd love to hear from you! Join us here: https://www.facebook.com/groups/481805558667334

BLOG

Learn more about happiness at work and life by visiting my blog at http://www.worklifesolutions.nz/category/latest. You'll find a variety of articles and tips about people pursuing their passion and strategies to help you pursue yours.

For information about products and workshops, or to ask me to come and speak at your workplace or conference, contact: cassandra@worklifesolutions.co.nz

PRESENTATIONS

For information about products and workshops, navigate to: http://www.worklifesolutions.nz/services-for-organisations/workshops-presentations.

To ask Cassandra to come and speak at your workplace or conference, contact: careerrescue@worklifesolutions.co.nz.

FOLLOW ME AND CONTINUE TO BE INSPIRED

www.twitter.com/gethappyatwork

www.instagram.com/midlife_career_rescue

www.facebook.com/worklifesolutions

www.pinterest.com/worklifenz

www.youtube.com/user/cassandragaisfordnz

"Do you know what you are? You are a marvel. You are unique. In all the years that have passed, there has never been another child like you. Your legs, your arms, your clever fingers, the way you move. You may become a Shakespeare, a Michelangelo, a Beethoven. You have the capacity for anything. Yes, you are a marvel."
~ Pablo Picasso, Spanish Artist

ACKNOWLEDGEMENTS

This book (and my new life) was made possible by the amazing generosity, open heartedness and wonderful friendship of so many people. Thank you!

Sir Edmund Hillary often said that even Mount Everest wasn't climbed alone. A great achievement or, in my case, a good book, is a product of collaboration. This project has, at times, loomed larger than the highest mountain in the world. I could not have persevered without the tremendous encouragement from a wealth of supportive and talented people.

To all the amazingly, interesting clients who have allowed me to help them over the years, and to the wonderful people who read my newspaper columns and wrote to me with their stories of reinvention—thank you. Your feedback, deep sharing, requests for help and inspired, courageous action, continues to inspire me.

I'd also like to say a special thanks to the staff at The Dominion Post newspaper who gave me my first break into published writing. This book would never have existed had they not acted on my suggestion that a careers column would be a great idea.

For over four years they gave me the encouragement and artistic freedom to write freely on a range of topics—all with the goal of helping encourage and inspire others.

I'm also grateful to the Health Editor of Marie Claire magazine who, after she had accepted a short article, said I had the bones of a good book and should write it.

My thanks also to my terrific friends and supporters. And of course I can never say thank you enough to my family, particularly my parents and grandparents, who have instilled me with such tremendous values and life skills.

My daughter, Hannah. I wish for you everything that your heart desires. Without you I doubt I would ever have accomplished all the things I have in my life.

Thank you.

FEEDBACK IS APPRECIATED

Thank you for purchasing and reading my book. I really hope you enjoyed it. Your feedback is important to me and I love hearing what you think and feel.

Please help me ensure this book reaches as many people like you who need a career rescue. Please leave me a REVIEW ON AMAZON

And if you'd like to be the first to know when other books in the series become available, follow this link to go to my pre-release page http://bit.ly/1PJ2uOg

Thank you so much!

ABOUT THE AUTHOR

Cassandra Gaisford is a #1 Amazon best-selling author, holistic energy psychologist, career counsellor and life coach. She also trains people who are passionate about making a difference in peoples' lives to be professional career and life coaches.

A corporate escapee, she now lives and works from her idyllic lifestyle property overlooking the Bay of Islands, in New Zealand.

Cassandra has been a bank teller, travel manager, recruitment consultant, outplacement consultant, EAP counsellor, human resources manager, leadership coach and change catalyst, and a wide range of other roles working in large multi-national corporations and not-for-profit organizations.

She is also a creative entrepreneur and has set up many businesses for herself, and for others - including an Employee Assistance Program provider wanting to add career counselling and coaching to their list of services.

She's a mid-lifer who wants more from her career than just go to work, grit her teeth and bare it. She wants to work with joy, passion, purpose and fulfilment—and she still wants to pay the bills! Every day she is grateful that she has achieved all of those desires—and more. Through her books and services she is looking forward to helping you achieve those things too.

Her journey and lessons learned are shared in her books, including, *Mid-life Career Rescue,* and *"How to Find Your Passion and Purpose.* Her other non-fiction books include *Happy at Work For Mid-Lifers.* She has also written a range of other titles that can be found on her website, http://www.worklifesolutions.co.nz/shop-intro

Cassandra is also an artist and author of historical art-related fiction. She loves all the arts, travelling, orchids and anything that is beautiful, inspiring and uplifting. Learn more about her on her blog, or connect with her on Facebook (http://www.facebook.com/worklifesolutions) and Twitter (http://twitter.com/gethappyatwork).

Made in the USA
Middletown, DE
04 March 2018